About KidCaps

KidCaps is an imprint of BookCaps™ that is just for kids! Each month BookCaps will be releasing several books in this exciting imprint. Visit are website or like us on Facebook to see more!

The Vietnam War

Soldiers jump off of a helicopter and run into battle during the Vietnam War[1]

---

[1] Image source: http://commons.wikimedia.org/wiki/Category:Battles_and_operations_of_the_Vietnam_War

Introduction

Nguyễn Văn Vien opened his eyes and saw nothing. It was pitch black outside and everything in his house was quiet. His parents and brothers must still be sleeping, so he would have to be careful not to make any noise as he got out of bed. Actually, Vien didn't know why he was awake. It was summertime, so if it was still dark outside then it must be early. Normally he had to wake up with the sun at around 6:30 to get an early start with his chores. As the oldest boy, it was his honor to feed the family chickens and to search for eggs every morning.

As he sat up and put his bare feet onto the cool earth of the floor, Vien was reminded that his family was not rich; they couldn't even afford a floor for the house. But they were one of the few families that could have eggs every day; other families could only afford to eat rice and vegetables, maybe a little bit of fish every now and then. But with sixteen hens and two roosters, the Nguyễn family gathered more eggs each week than they could possibly eat. Although his mother wanted to sell the extra eggs at the market in the nearby village of Con Thien, his father almost always ended up giving them to one of their hungry neighbors.

Vien listened carefully and noticed that everything was remarkably quiet outside. Normally he could hear the hum of insects from the jungle surrounding his family's house, and sometimes the two roosters would try to out crow each other. But tonight he heard nothing. No crowing, no buzzing, just silence.

Then it began.

The sounds seemed to come from everywhere all at once. He felt like his bed was being lifted from the ground, and the world around had exploded into a million billion fiery pieces. Where moments before there had been blackness and tranquility he now saw bright lights and heard screaming words that he couldn't understand. The blankets under him seemed hot, and he realized that they were on fire. Rolling onto the floor away from his bed he tried to yell for his family, but thick black smoke filled his lungs and made him start coughing. He backed up towards the space where seconds ago a wall had been.

A strong pair of hands grabbed him under his armpits and pulled him out and away from his house. Without even seeing who was holding him Vien starting hitting and kicking. Surely he was being kidnapped by the Northern Communists. He had heard that they liked to take boys around his age, which was twelve, and force them to be a part of their army. But no matter how hard his bare feet clawed at the soft dirt or how fiercely his little fists hit the thick black hands holding him, he was pulled further and further away from his house and family.

To his right, he saw two men arguing. They were both dressed in green, and Vien realized that they must be the Americans he had heard about who had been fighting in the other villages. He hadn't actually seen an American soldier before. One soldier pushed the other and pointed at the house. The second one shook his head and pointed at his chest.

Vien couldn't imagine what they were fighting, and anyways it didn't matter right now. His house was being eaten by the flames, and he thought that he could hear his little brother crying over the roaring fire. The soldier who had dragged him out set him down and went running back towards the fire. But the flames were too hot for him to go in and the water well was way away on the other side of the hill. There was nothing to be done. The fire could not be stopped. His family could not be saved.

Vien got up and started to run to the house, to find his parents and his brothers and to at least try to get them out. But the big same soldier that had carried him before now put his arms out and held Vien back. The heat from the inferno burnt Vien's cheeks as he finally got enough breath to scream out in pain and sadness. The soldier picked him up and carried him away, Vien looking over his soldier and shrieking, crying, not understanding. The other two soldiers were still arguing, and their voices were getting louder and louder. Although Vien could not understand the words, he got the idea. One of the men was responsible for the fire, and the other was mad at him for it. Three more soldiers came from the other side of the house. Vien looked at them with wet eyes, and they looked away. They said something to the big black soldier holding him and then shook their heads. One walked away from the group, put one hand against a tree, and started to throw up in the bushes.

Vien was all alone now. He didn't know what had happened or why, but he was suddenly sure of one thing: he had nobody now. The big soldier holding him put him down onto the ground and knelt before him. His tone was soft as he said something, and Vien could see that the soldier was sad too. He rubbed the top of Vien's head and pointed up to the sky, which was beginning to lighten as the sun rose. At first he didn't see anything but soon he heard a steady *thump thumpthump* and saw a helicopter come up over the horizon. He looked back at the soldier who nodded his head.

As the helicopter lifted a few minutes later, Vien felt strange and sad about what had happened. He felt guilty for enjoying the ride, but a thick knot quickly developed in his stomach as the helicopter went higher and higher. He could see his house, still burning, but he could also see lots of other houses burning on the mountainside. Like stars in the night sky, dozens of fires raged in the dark jungle below. Vien could only imagine how many other boys like him had lost everything. He covered his face with his eyes and wept.

How do you feel when you read the story of Nguyễn Văn Vien? Does it make you sad to read about his suffering and his fear? The truth is that lots of kids just like Vien lost their homes, their families, and even their lives during the Vietnam War. It was a sad time and millions of people's lives were forever changed by it. Have you heard much about the Vietnam War? Do you know someone who fought in it? In this book, we will take a closer look at this war that got the whole world's attention. We will find out what happened to the kids like Vien and why there was so much confusion and even disagreement among the troops fighting in the war. What else can you expect to see in this book?

We will look at what led up to the actual war. Although the United States did not officially start fighting until 1964, there had been conflict and violence in the country of Vietnam for over twenty years, since World War Two. We will learn what led to the United States' involvement and how the fighting began.

Then we will learn about *why* the war happened. Although the war was actually a civil war between the Vietnamese people, it ended up involving soldiers and civilians from China, the Soviet Union, the United States, Laos, and Cambodia. Why did so many people end up fighting? As we will see in this section, each country had its own motive, and its own reasons to get involved.

The following section will tell us more about some of the things that happened during the war itself. We will see the unique tactics used by both sides and whether or not they worked. In one case, the tactic of using statistics would have awful consequences for both sides. We will also see some of the problems faced by the soldiers fighting the war and some of the effects the battle had on average Americans living back in the U.S.

Then we will see what it was like to be a kid back then. Whether you lived in the U.S. or in the middle of the war, you would have had to think about the fighting every day. Would you be surprised to learn that not everyone thought that the war was a good idea? And then the next section will talk about how the war finally ended and then we'll see what happened afterwards. From the effects on the people fighting, on the civilians, and on the countries themselves, the Vietnam War still affects millions of people today.

Are you ready to learn more? While parts of this book may make us a little sad, especially the parts that talk about the violence, try to look at each section from two different viewpoints: what the Americans were thinking and what the Vietnamese people were thinking. At the end of the book, we will ask some tough questions, questions that a lot of people still can't agree on today. They will have to do with whether or not it was right to fight the war and whether or not things could have been done differently.

Keep reading and together we will learn more about the Vietnam War.

Chapter 1: What Led Up to the Vietnam War?

Although there was fighting in Vietnam for many years, when we talk about "The Vietnam War" we are specifically talking about the time when American soldiers were fighting against Communist forces in Vietnam and its surrounding countries (including Laos and Cambodia). Although there had been American troops and American equipment helping the South Vietnamese fight since 1962, the real war between American soldiers and the Communist troops began in March 1965 and ended in the spring of 1973. But how did American soldiers end up halfway around the globe participating in a small Asian country's civil war? It all started shortly after World War Two ended.

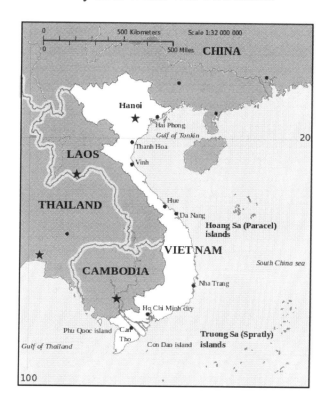

A map of Vietnam and some nearby countries[2]

Ever since the late 1800s, the country of France had been in control of several countries in Southeast Asia, including Vietnam. The whole region was called Indochina, and included the countries of Vietnam, Laos, and Cambodia. While the French were busy fighting against the Germans in Europe during World War Two, Japan aggressively invaded the area and took over some land from Vietnam. The Japanese began to boss around the people who lived there. But when the war ended, and Japan went back to their island, the people of Vietnam decided that they didn't want *anyone* to be in charge of them anymore and began to fight against the French.

The northern part of the country thought that the best thing for Vietnam would be to be an independent Communist state. A political party called the ViệtMinh Party was then organized by a man named Ho Chi Minh. Ho Chi Minh was inspired by the Communist takeovers of China and the Soviet Union, and he thought that the Communist way of life would help his people in Vietnam. During a time when there wasn't enough food to eat because no one had any money to buy it, Ho Chi Minh and his ViệtMinh party broke into the warehouses like Robin Hood and gave the rice they stole to the hungry Vietnamese people. Because he put food on their tables, many Vietnamese citizens began to support the Communist ViệtMinh party. In 1945, he seized the northern city of Hanoi and made it the capital of a new country, the Democratic republic of Vietnam (North Vietnam).

The fighting got worse and worse between the Vietnamese and the French, and the French were finally defeated at the Battle of Dien Bien Phu that ended on May 7, 1954. The French had few troops after all of the violence of World War Two, so although they tried to hold onto their power in Vietnam the fighting obviously didn't go too well for them. The international community decided that the French should leave Vietnam in the hands of the Vietnamese. The country would be temporarily divided into two halves, North and South, with a border at the 17th Parallel. It was also decided that the country would have a special election in 1956 to decided how best to reunite the two halves.

The French obeyed and left the country in 1954 but made sure that the southern part stayed under the control of French-educated Emperor BảoĐại. Although the emperor had been around for a while, he was not immensely popular. NgôĐinhDiệm, a politician who became popular with the United States because he hated Communists, became the Prime Minister and then forced the emperor to leave the country. A special election was held, and in 1955, NgôĐinhDiệm became the first president of the Republic of Vietnam (South Vietnam).

The country was now officially split into two halves, north and south, with two different leaders who had different ways of thinking and yet who both wanted the country to be united under one government. The problem was that everyone couldn't agree on what sort of government that should be. Can you see how things were starting to get complicated in Vietnam?

What kind of President was NgôĐinhDiệm? Well, he was the sort of man who did everything possible to get his way, even if it meant breaking the rules and hurting other people. While the United States liked him because he hated Communism, they quickly realized that President NgôĐinhDiệm was a brutal dictator. Instead of trying to unite his country peacefully as the international community had told him to, he cancelled the vote and began to kill everyone that did not agree with him. Instead of letting the people decide wither they wanted a communist government or a democratic government, he rounded up everyone who supported the North Vietnamese Communists and had them put in jail, tortured, and killed. It is believed that soon after becoming president NgôĐinhDiệm killed over 100,000 people this way.

NgôĐinhDiệm was also distrusting of anyone who wasn't related to him, and his government was corrupt. That means that a lot of people didn't do their jobs and that they kept lots of money for themselves instead of sharing it with the poor citizens who they were supposed to be helping. As a result of seeing so much suffering, groups of citizens in South Vietnam got together and formed an organization called the National Liberation Front (the NLF). In Vietnamese, the name of this organization was called Việtcộng. The Việtcộng, or NLF, was supposedly made up of both communist soldiers from the north and democratic soldiers from the south. They were united by the common goal of uniting Vietnam together and getting rid of bad leaders. However, the United States felt that the Việtcộng didn't represent all of the Vietnamese people and that it was only a tool for the Northern Communists.

The fighting between the Việtcộng and the South Vietnam military got more and more frequent during the late 1950s. From 1957-1959, the fighting escalated from small skirmishes to full out battles between large groups of soldiers. Back in 1954, President Dwight D. Eisenhower had promised to help the South out as much he could without actually doing any of the fighting, so he ended up sending over 900 soldiers as "advisors" to help the South fight their war against the North.

In January of 1961 John F. Kennedy became President of the United States. It was clear to everyone that the situation was getting more and more serious in Vietnam and that the South was likely to be taken over by the Communist North. Because the U.S. Government had promised to help the South Vietnamese government, President Kennedy was urged by his advisors to send more people to Vietnam. By 1962, some 9,000 American troops were in South Vietnam to provide training to Vietnamese troops there, and by 1963, there were 16,000 troops stationed there. There was continued fighting between the North and the South, but the Americans saw no reason to get any more involved than they already were.

In November of 1963, all of that changed.

On November 2, NgôĐìnhDiệm was assassinated by a group of his fellow countrymen, and less than three weeks later President John F. Kennedy was also assassinated. Two of the primary figures in the struggle to keep South Vietnam out of the hands of the Communist forces had died, and there was absolute chaos in both governments. Although President Kennedy had signed an order to withdraw troops from Vietnam his successor, President Lyndon B. Johnson, expanded the number of troops and work to be done there.

Lyndon B. Johnson was sworn in as President on November 22, 1963[3]

[3] Image source: http://en.wikipedia.org/wiki/Lyndon_B._Johnson

There was no one leader to replace NgôĐìnhDiệm in South Vietnam, and several more attempts were made by various groups trying to take control of the situation. Finally, General Nguyen Khanh took control in 1964.

Although he increased the amount of troops in Vietnam, President Johnson did not see the situation there as important, and he preferred to focus his attention of other matters. But soon he would be forced to rethink how he was dealing with this small country in Southeast Asia.

On August 2, 1964, the USS *Maddox*, a United States destroyer, was patrolling the waters off the coast of North Vietnam in an area called the Gulf of Tonkin when suddenly it reported that it had been fired upon by three North Vietnamese torpedo boats. They fired back, sinking one of the North Vietnamese ships, and several planes went out to investigate and protect the *Maddox*. Two days later, on August 4, there were more reports of American ships narrowly dodging North Vietnamese torpedoes.

Now President Johnson had to decide what to do. Instead of simply provide advice and guidance to South Vietnamese troops fighting a civil war, American soldiers had been fired upon. They had been trying to maintain internationally recognized territory, and now it looked like the North was becoming more aggressive than ever.

On August 5, President Johnson went before Congress and gave a speech that included the following words:

> "Our policy in southeast Asia has been consistent and unchanged since 19554. I summarized it on June 2 in four simple propositions:
> 1. America keeps her word. Here as elsewhere, we must and shall honor our commitments.
> 2. The issue is the future of Southeast Asia as a whole. A threat to any nation in that region is a threat to all, and a threat to us.
> 3. Our purpose is peace. We have no military, political, or territorial ambitions in the area.
> 4. This is not just a jungle war, but a struggle for freedom on every front of human activity. Our military and economic assistance to South Vietnam and Laos in particular has the purpose of helping these countries to repel aggression and strengthen their independence.
> The threat to the free nations of Southeast Asia has long been clear. The North Vietnamese regime has constantly sought to take over South Vietnam and Laos. This Communist regime has violated the Geneva accords for Vietnam. It has systematically conducted a campaign of subversion, which includes the direction, training, and supply of personnel and arms for the conduct of guerrilla warfare in South Vietnamese territory."[4]

In that important speech, called the Gulf of Tonkin Resolution, President Johnson asked for the support of Congress in giving more aid to South Vietnam. Although there was no specific mention of war, the President knew that Congress would let him do whatever he thought was appropriate.

As more American troops arrived in Vietnam, the number of supporters of the Việtcộng also increased, numbering about 100,000 by the end of 1964. The Việtcộng saw more American troops as a threat to the independence of Vietnam were ready to fight against any new soldiers that arrived. On March 2, 1965, some barracks (the place where soldiers live) were attacked and the U.S. responded by bombing the enemy. Six days later 3,500 Marines were sent to South Vietnam to fight.

[4] Quotation source: http://www.pbs.org/wgbh/amex/vietnam/psources/ps_tonkingulf.html

The Vietnam War had officially begun.

Chapter 2: Why Did the Vietnam War Happen?

When you look at that question, "Why did the Vietnam War happen," you might think that there is a simple answer. However as we will see in this section, the Vietnam War was fought largely due to miscommunication. The Vietnamese didn't understand what the Americans wanted, and the Americans didn't understand what the Vietnamese wanted. And the end result was that over three million people from many different countries died. As we talk about the "why" of the Vietnam War, don't be afraid to ask yourself or any adults you know some of the tough questions, like "Did this war have to happen?" and "Could it have been avoided?" Let's learn more.

We will start by looking at the war and the events leading up to it through the eyes of the Vietnamese people. Do you remember why Ho Chi Minh formed the ViệtMinh Party in the first place? While he and his partners certainly agreed with the Communist way of thinking and doing things, their party name specifically mentioned their greater goal. The name "ViệtMinh" was short for "Việt Nam ĐộcLậpĐồng Minh Hội", which in English means "The League for the Independence of Vietnam". The reason that Ho Chi Minh and the others formed their Communist political party was to fight for an independent Vietnam. After decades of being bossed around first by the French and then by the Japanese, the Vietnamese people wanted to rule for themselves.

When NgôĐìnhDiệm became President and started to treat his fellow Vietnamese cruelly, we saw that a group called the Việtcộng was formed. In English, the name Việtcộng meant National Liberation Front. Because "liberation" has to do with freeing something that is being held like a prisoner, we can see again that the Vietnamese people were not necessarily interested in Communism or Democracy; they simply wanted their country to be free. As the United States began to support different leaders (first NgôĐìnhDiệm and then others). many Vietnamese felt like it was history repeating itself all over again. They felt that foreign nations were coming in again to tell them how to run their country.

Now imagine how many of the common Vietnamese citizens felt as they saw more and more troops come from the United States and move into their neighborhoods and villages. Do you think that they would have been happy to see these strange men dressed in green uniforms or would they have been afraid? The truth is that instead of seeing the American soldiers as people who were there to help them to restore the peace, most Vietnamese (including those from the South) viewed the Americans as big bullies who just wanted to take over Vietnam and to become the new bosses. For that reason, many chose to fight against the American soldiers.

This way of thinking can be seen in a conversation years later between two of the important men of the Vietnam War: U.S. Secretary of Defense Robert McNamara and Vietnamese Foreign Minister NguyễnCơThạch.

Robert McNamara (on the right) with President Johnson during an important meeting[5]

During an interview years later, Robert McNamara mentioned how surprised he was when he learned what the Vietnamese had been fighting for all along. He said:

> "In the case of Vietnam, we didn't know them well enough to empathize. And there was total misunderstanding as a result. They believed that we had simply replaced the French as a colonial power, and we were seeking to subject South and North Vietnam to our colonial interests, which was absolutely absurd. And we, we saw Vietnam as an element of the Cold War. Not what they saw it as: a civil war.
>
> There aren't many examples in which you bring two former enemies together, at the highest levels, and discuss what might have been. I formed the hypothesis that each of us could have achieved our objectives without the terrible loss of life. And I wanted to test that by going to Vietnam. The former Foreign Minister of Vietnam, a wonderful man named Thạch said, "You're totally wrong. We were fighting for our independence. You were fighting to enslave us."
>
> "Do you mean to say it was not a tragedy for you, when you lost 3 million 4 hundred thousand Vietnamese killed, which on our population base is the equivalent of 27 million Americans? What did you accomplish? You didn't get any more than we were willing to give you at the beginning of the war. You could have had the whole damn thing: independence, unification."
>
> "Mr. McNamara, You must never have read a history book. If you'd had, you'd know we weren't pawns of the Chinese or the Russians. McNamara, didn't you know that? Don't you understand that we have been fighting the Chinese for 1000 years? We were fighting for our independence. And we would fight to the last man. And we were determined to do so. And no amount of bombing, no amount of U.S. pressure would ever have stopped us." "[6]

Do you understand that important conversation? The Vietnamese Foreign Minister said that the Vietnamese people were fighting for their independence. When they saw the U.S. soldiers come marching in with their guns, they felt the same way as the American colonists did back in 1776 when they saw the British redcoats come marching in with their guns. The Vietnamese thought that they were fighting for their freedom.

[5] Image source: http://commons.wikimedia.org/wiki/Category:Robert_McNamara
[6] Quotation source: http://www.errolmorris.com/film/fow_transcript.html

But what did the Americans think that they were fighting for?

The Americans thought that they were fighting to contain Communism, to keep it from spreading any further than it already had. After watching the Soviet Union and China be overthrown by Communist soldiers, the American government worried that other countries might become Communist too, and that all of them would get together and form a super nation that would start another world war and take over the world. Like dominoes all lined up in a row, they thought that if one country in Southeast Asia became Communist then others might also. President Johnson, in several private phone calls to Defense Secretary Robert McNamara, explained how he thought something like that could happen:

> "I would say that we have a commitment to Vietnamese freedom. We could pull out of there, the dominoes would fall, and that part of the world would go to the Communists."

> "We have declared war on tyranny and aggression. If this little nation goes down the drain and can't maintain her independence, ask yourself what's going to happen to all these other little nations."[7]

This theory, called the "Domino Theory" was made popular earlier by President Eisenhower and continued to affect the decisions made by presidents throughout the Korean and Vietnam Wars. By sending troops to fight in Vietnam, the Americans felt like they were genuinely fighting against Communism. And because China and the Soviet Union were giving supplies to the North Vietnamese, for the Americans this war turned into part of the Cold War with the Soviets.

Like dominos in a line that fall one after another, President Johnson was afraid that lots of countries would become Communist if Vietnam was allowed to fall[8]

[7] Quotation source: http://www.4rrooms.com/myhow_transcript.html
[8] Image source: http://insureblog.blogspot.com/2012/07/dominos-part-deux.html

Can you see how this confusion totally changed the war? What do you think would have happened if the people involved stopped for a few minutes to try and figure out why the other side was acting a certain way or why they were doing certain things? Do you think that so many people would have died?

Defense Secretary Robert McNamara explained that the very cause of the United States sending more troops to Vietnam to fight, the Gulf of Tonkin Resolution, was also the result of a big misunderstanding. It turns out that U.S. ships were not attacked by North Vietnamese boats on August 4 as they had told everyone. McNamara said:

> "It was just confusion, and events afterwards showed that our judgment that we'd been attacked that day was wrong. It didn't happen. And the judgment that we'd been attacked on August 2nd was right. We had been, although that was disputed at the time. So we were right once and wrong once.
>
> Ultimately, President Johnson authorized bombing in response to what he thought had been the second attack. It hadn't occurred, but that's irrelevant to the point I'm making here. He authorized the attack on the assumption it had occurred, and his belief that it was a conscious decision on the part of the North Vietnamese political and military leaders to escalate the conflict and an indication they would not stop short of winning.
>
> We were wrong, but we had in our minds a mindset that led to that action. And it carried such heavy costs. We see incorrectly or we see only half of the story at times."[9]

As Robert McNamara said, there was a certain "mindset", or way of thinking, that many people in the United States government had at that time. They wanted to fight Communism, and they wanted to win a war. After having lost the Battle of the Bay of Pigs in Cuba and after having problems with the Soviets' building a wall in Berlin, the United States felt like it had a lousy reputation in the world. They were looking for a chance to be the heroes again, and when the civil war in Vietnam broke out and it looked like the Communist party might win, the United States thought it was their chance to ride in and save the day.

But as we saw earlier, the Vietnamese did not think they needed help from anyone else. They wanted to decide for themselves how to run the country and anyone who got involved would have a fight on their hands. The Vietnam War was actually just a civil war, but because of miscommunication and strong opinions, it quickly became a terrible conflict that would eventually kill over three million people. Do you think it could have gone differently? What would you have done if you had been there?

---

[9] Quotation source: http://www.errolmorris.com/film/fow_transcript.html

Chapter 3: What Happened During the Vietnam War?

The Vietnam War was a confusing time for almost everyone involved. As we already mentioned, the two sides didn't understand each other and weren't exactly sure what their enemy wanted to achieve. But the Vietnam War saw some interesting things happen for the first time ever on the battlefield. There was a focus on **attrition** and not on gaining more territory; there were **problems within the ranks** of the American soldiers, and many people back in the United States thought that the war created too much **controversy**. Let's look at each of those special circumstances one by one.

First, the United States did not have the same goals as most armies did during previous wars: to try to move their men forward and to conquer more land. From the very beginning, American soldiers were sure that the North Vietnamese were remarkably few in number. So instead of moving forward into North Vietnam to fight them, the Americans decided on a war of **attrition**. Attrition has to do with losing something a little bit at a time. The idea was that American soldiers would form a kind of "wall" in South Vietnam and then let the North Vietnamese come to them. As time went by, the Americans would win most of the battles, and the North Vietnamese would eventually run out of soldiers and ammunition to fight the war. In the meantime, the South Vietnamese would take care of the Việtcộng in their territory, behind the "wall" of Americans.

The first phase of the plan was initiated in March of 1965 and was called Operation Rolling Thunder. Along with stopping the movement of soldiers from the North to the South, Operation Rolling Thunder had the goal of making sure that North Vietnam stopped supported the Việtcộng fighters in the South. Lots of different types of bombs were dropped on North Vietnam to make this happen. There were bombs to destroy anti-aircraft missiles and bombs for destroying military targets and even bombs for oil storage warehouses. But no matter how many thousands of pounds of explosives were dropped in North Vietnam, the Americans didn't see any real difference. The North Vietnamese had prepared well and were even able to set traps for the flying bombers and shoot lots of them down.

As the focus began to move more and more onto the ground war that the soldiers were fighting in South Vietnam, different types of bombs were used. During a special plan called Operation Ranch Hand, strong chemicals were sprayed over parts of South Vietnam. The chemicals would kill all of the plants in the area.

A United States helicopter spraying Agent Orange over the jungles of Vietnam[10]

Why did the United States want to kill the plants in South Vietnam? Well, the soldiers simply weren't used to having to fight and move through so many plants. It gave the Việtcộng so many places to hide and made sure that they had plenty of food. So by killing the plants, the Americans hoped that the Việtcộng wouldn't be able to hide anymore, the battles would be easier, and that eventually they would have to give up because of not having food.

The Americans also hoped to force most of the Vietnamese to go away from the war zone and into the large cities. Why? Well, as we will see later, the Việtcộng did not wear military uniforms: they looked just like everyone else. Because the soldiers couldn't always tell who was an innocent civilian and who was a trained soldier waiting to kill them, it made the stress levels high. The chemicals dropped on the jungles should make all that easier.

Unfortunately, the chemicals that were dropped (including one called Agent Orange) had terrible side effects. Any Vietnamese people were born with diseases, many babies died in their mother's wombs, and the American soldiers themselves got cancer from Agent Orange after the war had finished. Although they may have helped the war effort a little bit, Agent Orange and the other chemicals dropped on the jungles of South Vietnam did a lot of harm to both the Vietnamese people and to the American soldiers.

The whole strategy of the war had to do with **attrition**, because the Americans believed that the North Vietnamese and the Việtcộng were small in number and that the war wouldn't last too long. However as the fighting went on, more and more Việtcộng kept popping up in South Vietnam and more and more North Vietnamese kept fighting strong for their country. In other words, no matter how many people died in the fighting, there were always more soldiers coming onto the battlefields. The idea of attrition wasn't working.

This was made especially clear on January 30, 1968. Three years after the bombing and fighting had started, the Americans were shocked when they saw a huge, well-organized attack carried out by the

North Vietnamese in multiple cities. Called the Tet Offensive ("Tet" was the Vietnamese word for the new year) it showed that the North Vietnamese and the Việtcộng weren't going anywhere and that they were still strong, still organized, and still ready to fight.

The city of Saigon was attacked severely during the Tet Offensive[11]

In other words, after three years, the Americans were still not anywhere near to winning the war. The strategy of using **attrition** to win the war was not working.

Other important factors in the Vietnam War were the **problems faced by the American soldiers** themselves. As we mentioned earlier, the Vietnam War was unlike all previous wars. The enemy did not wear special uniforms or march together in large armies. They dressed the same as the innocent civilians and would often hide with civilian families pretending to be just another villager. Then when the American soldiers weren't looking they would shoot them down or throw a grenade.

The American soldiers learned to not trust any Vietnamese people that they saw. They thought that the only way to stay alive was to shoot first and ask questions later. As a result, a lot of innocent people died. But it got even worse. As part of their strategy of attrition, the U.S. government focused a lot on the numbers. They wanted to know how many bombs were dropped, how many bullets were fired, and how many enemy soldiers were killed. The American forces on the ground felt a lot of pressure to shoot more people so that the reports looked better, and so they often threw grenades, used flamethrowers, and shot their guns without making sure that the targets were actually enemies, and not innocent villagers.

A tragedy in the South Vietnamese city of Mỹ Lai is a good example of what was happening on the ground during the Vietnam War. On March 16, 1968, American soldiers marched into this small village to check for Việtcộng soldiers. They had been told that all of the villagers would be at the market buying food and that anyone who was still in the village when the Americans arrived must be Việtcộng fighters. The soldiers went in ready to fight.

After suffering at the hands of the North Vietnamese and the Việtcộng fighters a few weeks before during the Tet Offensive, the American soldiers wanted revenge, and wanted to make sure that no more attacks like that could happen again. Their commanders told them that everyone that they came across was sure to be either a Communist or a Communist supporter. And when the soldiers asked about women and children, they were told that *everyone* in that village was a potential threat, even the women and children.

When they entered the village in the morning, the soldiers looked for hiding soldiers in the houses of the elderly villagers. A few villagers were shot, and that made the soldiers start to go kind of crazy. They started shooting animals and people and killing them with grenades and bayonets. They pushed groups of people together into ditches and shot them with machine guns. Women and children were shot and shoved into ditches. When an American helicopter pilot saw what was happening he landed his helicopter between his fellow soldiers and the Vietnamese villagers who were running for their lives and rescued the Vietnamese villagers, who ended up being a group of women, children, and old men.

When they later investigated what had happened at Mỹ Lai, there were no weapons, no young soldiers, and no threat of any kind. In other words, those American soldiers had killed all of those Vietnamese villagers for nothing: they were South Vietnamese supporters who the Americans were supposed to be helping. Because of poor communication, frustration over the difficult war, and an incorrect mindset, 347 innocent Vietnamese citizens died that day.

This is a picture taken of some of the My Lai citizens who were later killed during the massacre[12]

The soldiers were fighting a difficult war, and incidents like this one (which came to be called the Mỹ Lai Massacre) made their job even harder. More Vietnamese joined the Việtcộng fighters as they saw the Americans as dangerous bullies who wanted to take away their freedom.

As the war kept progressing, the U.S. government began to wonder whether or not it could be won. They began to wonder whether or not they should keep sending over troops and equipment. All this doubt made the soldiers feel like they were risking their lives every day for nothing and some even began to feel like they were fighting a pointless war. During the final years of the Vietnam War, soldiers started to use drugs, became more violent, deserted the Army, and would even kill their superior officers on purpose. It was a sad time both for Americans and for the Vietnamese.

Another important circumstance that made the Vietnam War unique was that back in the United States, the Vietnam War had created a lot of **controversy**. Although at first a large number of Americans agreed that it was a good idea to send troops to help the Vietnamese fight the Communists, as time went by it started to look like the whole thing had been a huge mistake. Groups of protestors began to demonstrate against the war and to make signs and shout about their opinions on college campuses across the country. Thousands of people marched in Washington D.C. asking the President to end the war. As more and more American soldiers came back and were interviewed about what the war was like, less Americans supported it.

[12] Image source: http://commons.wikimedia.org/wiki/File:My_Lai_massacre_woman_and_children.jpg

The protests started to divide the country into two halves: those who supported the war and those who didn't. The two sides couldn't understand each other and often ended up fighting between themselves. Some of the college campus protests turned deadly. On May 4, 1970, at Kent State University in Ohio, student protestors who were speaking out against the war and the terrible violence against the Vietnamese people were shot at by National Guard soldiers. Four students were killed, and nine more were wounded.

National Guard soldiers shot tear gas and bullets at the Kent State protestors[13]

All across the country, students went on strike and hundreds of colleges and universities shut down. The country now had to make a decision as to what they were going to do about the war in Vietnam. Never before had the nation become so deeply divided about an issue, and never before had Americans killed Americans over a war that was happening thousands of miles away on the other side of the world.

As more reports surfaced about the awful behavior of American soldiers, many also learned about how President Nixon ordered illegal bombing raids on and an invasion of Vietnam's neighbor Cambodia. This only made the protests increase in size and scope, and President Nixon began secretly recording conversations in order to find out who was the on revealing confidential information. This habit would later get him in trouble during something called the Watergate scandal.

By the early 1970s, things were looking bad in Vietnam, bad in the United States, and bad in the White House. Something had to change.

---

[13] Image source: http://www.kentstate1970.org/

Chapter 4: What Was It Like to Be a Kid During the Vietnam War?

After seeing all of the sad things that happened during the Vietnam War, can you imagine being a kid back then? In the introduction, we saw the story of Nguyễn Văn Vien. The truth is that there were many kids just like his who lost their families, their homes, and even their lives. Because of soldiers who acted crazy, because of miscommunications, and because of accidents, thousands and thousands of Vietnamese civilians died at the hands of American soldiers.

If you were a kid living in Vietnam, you would probably have been scared the whole time. Not only was there a civil war going on, which was bad enough, but now there were foreign troops dropping bombs, throwing grenades, and shooting guns in your home country. If you were a kid, especially if you were a boy, you would be afraid that someday one of those soldiers might get confused and shoot you because they thought that you were a soldier. Or you might be afraid to go to sleep just in case the enemy came at night and attacked your village.

Just as the Americans were confused about whom their friends were and whom their enemies were, the Vietnamese themselves also didn't always know whom to trust. The kids often got stuck in the middle and were scared of everyone. Worse yet, they often didn't understand what was going on. They weren't the only ones who didn't know why the Americans were killing the Vietnamese.

Back in the United States, American kids watched their older brothers and neighbors go off to war; and they saw how some of them never came home. Over 50,000 young American soldiers died in Vietnam during the war and it made a lot of families sad. Can you imagine watching the news every night and seeing reports of the fighting? Can you imagine going to the funerals of guys you knew and watching their parents cry? Do you think that you would have understood everything that was going on? Would you have agreed with it?

Kids in the U.S. saw the world around them get divided into two groups: those who supported the war and those who didn't. But sometimes, families were divided into two groups also. Mothers and fathers got into arguments about the war, and kids disagreed with parents. It was a scary time, a time when lots of people fought and argued and said mean things. Also, imagine what it would be like to see the protestors. Protestors often marched down the streets so everyone could see them, but unlike other parades where everyone was smiling, these protest marches often had a lot of yelling, and some ended with people on the ground, injured and crying.

Being a kid back then (whether in the United States or in Vietnam) would have been scary and sometimes it would have seemed like the world was losing its mind.

Chapter 5: How Did the Vietnam War End?

Most wars end with a huge battle or with parades or with a big victory. But the Vietnam War didn't end like that at all. As time went by, the United States government saw that the war could not be won. There were too many enemy soldiers, too many Americans were dying, and the county no longer supported the war effort. Then, the Tet Offensive in 1968 and something similar called the Easter Offensive in 1972 showed that North Vietnamese soldiers and the Việtcộng were nowhere near done fighting.

Secret negotiations were made between the U.S. and North Vietnam, and it was decided to stop sending new soldiers to Vietnam and to bring the soldiers already there back home. On March 29, 1973, the last soldier left Vietnam and returned to the United States.

The Vietnam War had claimed so many lives, yet it ended the same way as it had started: two halves of Vietnam separated at the 17th parallel fighting a civil war. After all the bombs, after all the guns, after all the death and crying, absolutely nothing had changed.

The Americans had been worried about the Communists taking over Southeast Asia if they didn't get involved. So were they right? What actually happened once the American soldiers left?

What happened after the Vietnam War ended?

After the Vietnam War ended, what Americans had feared would happen actually did happen: South Vietnam was taken over by Communist forces in April, 1975. That same year Laos and Cambodia were also taken over by Communist parties. It looked like the Domino Theory had been right and that Southeast Asia now belonged to the Soviet Union and China.

Only that's not what happened at all.

While those three countries had civil wars and became Communist (Cambodia later changed its mind and became a constitutional monarchy with a King and a Prime Minister) none of them wanted to be under the control of the Soviet Union or China. Even though they chose Communism, they also chose to remain independent from all foreign governments. So even though the Communist ideas spread from one country to another, there was no creation of a new superpower that tried to take over the world; no new international government to threaten global peace.

In other words, the Domino Theory had been wrong. Even if the United States had not gotten involved, and even if all those people wouldn't have died, things probably would have turned out the exact same as they are today.

As the American soldiers who had fought in Vietnam were sent home, they found that no one actually treated them as heroes. Instead of big parades and special dinners in their honor, and visits to the White House, many veterans found that no one was happy with them. Those who had been against the war called them "baby killers" and those who had supported the war were upset with the soldiers and blamed them for not winning it.

Many of the soldiers also suffered from the things that they had seen and heard. About one in every six soldiers suffered some sort of emotional problem after the war. Some people called it "shell shock" and others called it Post Traumatic Stress Disorder (PTSD). It made it hard for soldiers to calm down. Sometimes they felt like they were still at war and that they might be shot at any moment. Because people didn't truly understand a lot about the human brain back then, many made fun of the soldiers and refused to give them jobs. It was not a nice homecoming present.

Over the next few decades international and economic relations were fixed between Vietnam and the United States. In 1982, a beautiful monument was put up in Washington D.C. to honor all those Americans who had died during the Vietnam War. 58,272 names are listed along with the years when they died.

A U.S. Marine looks at the names of fallen soldiers at the Vietnam Veterans Memorial[14]

---

[14] Image source: http://en.wikipedia.org/wiki/Vietnam_Veterans_Memorial

Conclusion

Although it's kind of sad to learn about the fighting and the suffering of the Vietnam War, it is important for each new generation to learn from the successes and failures of the previous one. Kids learn from parents and parents learn from grandparents. What do you think: was the Vietnam War a success or a failure? A lot of people agree: the Vietnam War should never have happened. Let's review some of the things that we learned in this book.

First, we looked at what led up to the actual war. Although the United States did not officially start fighting until 1964, there had been conflict and violence in the country of Vietnam for over twenty years, since World War Two. The French and the Japanese had dominated Vietnam and the Vietnamese people were tired of it. They decided to fight back, and the Vietnam War happened. We saw how more and more troops we sent to train the South Vietnamese soldiers but how the fighting actually started after the Gulf of Tonkin incident.

Then we learned about *why* the war happened. Although the war was actually a civil war between the Vietnamese people, it ended up involving soldiers and civilians from China, the Soviet Union, the United States, Laos, and Cambodia. Why did so many people end up fighting? As we saw in this section, each country had its own motive, and its own reasons to get involved, but most of it had to do with poor communication. Everybody misunderstood what the other side wanted. Because of the lack of communication, friends became enemies and no one knew who to trust.

The following section told us more about some of the things that happened during the war itself. We saw the unique tactic of attrition used by the Americans and the secret warfare carried out by the Việtcộng. We also saw how the use of statistics had awful consequences for both sides because it made American soldiers more eager to shoot first and ask questions later. We also saw some of the problems faced by the soldiers fighting the war (like not knowing who their enemy was and who their friend was) and some of the effects the battles had on average Americans living back in the U.S., including the protests at Kent State and other universities.

We also looked at what it was like to be a kid back then. Whether you lived in the U.S. or in the middle of the war, you would have had to think about the fighting every day. Were you surprised to learn that not everyone thought that the war was a good idea? And then the next section talked about how the war finally ended. We saw how the U.S. government simply decided to remove the soldiers, realizing that the war could never be won. We then saw what happened afterwards, from the PTSD of the soldiers to the Vietnam Veterans Memorial.

From the effects on the people fighting, on the civilians, and on the countries themselves, the Vietnam War still affects millions of people today. What about you? Did you learn something new about the Vietnam War from reading this book? We sure hope so. And we hope that you have also learned how important it is to ask question. Because the right questions weren't asked before, during, and after the war, a lot of bad decisions were made that led to the suffering of millions of people.

The Vietnam War ended almost forty years ago, but the lessons we can learn will help us far into the future.

The Gulf War
A History Just for Kids

The *U.S.S. San Jacinto* was one of the first ships to fire a missile during the Gulf War[15]

---

[15] Image source: http://en.wikipedia.org/wiki/File:USSSanJacintoCG-56.jpg

Introduction

Tommy Johnson checked the settings for what seemed like the one hundredth time that morning. He couldn't believe that after so many hours of classes, of tests, and of drill after drill, the time had finally come for him and his crew to do what they had been trained to do: to fire a missile at the enemy in a time of war.

It was January 17, 1991, and Tommy Johnson and his men were serving on the *U.S.S. San Jacinto* in the Persian Gulf, near the countries of Kuwait and Iraq. There had been talk for some weeks about United States military action in the area, and an important deadline set by the United Nations had come and gone without anything truly changing. He and his men had been preparing for this moment for days, and now the opportunity had finally come for them to fire a brand new weapon that had never before been used during wartime: the Tomahawk cruise missile. It was called a "smart" missile by the people who made it.

Tommy Johnson was a petty officer and was the one responsible for making sure that the guidance system worked correctly on the missile. Unlike other types of bombs that were dropped from airplanes and just landed wherever, this new type of missile used satellites and onboard computers in order to find out where it was and in order to follow a pre-programmed flight path to the target. The goal was to make sure that only the enemy soldiers were hit by the missiles and not innocent civilians.

With the members of his small team each looking at different parts of the missile, Tommy could feel the excitement in the air. Here was their chance to stop the bad guys and to help the innocent. They were going to see if all of their hard work during the past months would pay off. If there were some sort of accident, and the missile didn't make it to the target or didn't launch correctly- well Tommy didn't even want to think about what might happen then. It wouldn't be good, he was sure of that.

To his right, Robert Atkinson, a fellow naval officer from Missouri, was checking to see that the outer structure of the missile was in good condition. The missile was long, over twenty feet including the booster, but Tommy was sure that Robert knew every detail of it like the back of his hand. Each missile cost almost one million dollars to make, so the men treated as it was: a supremely precious piece of cargo. Some of his other team members looked at the boosters, some checked the "payload" (as the actual bomb was called) and others double-checked the platform that would be used to launch the missile. Everything was looking good.

Above deck, Tommy knew that the rest of the crew of the *U.S.S. San Jacinto* would be anxious to see the launch. Because the missile would be launched from the front part of the ship, most of the crew would be gathered far away from the action on the rear helicopter pad to watch the missile go up into the air. Tommy verified the coordinates for the target: an Iraqi Air Force base with several fighters and large reserve fuel tanks. It was hoped that the Tomahawk would be able to destroy the planes and keep them from getting into the air during the coming weeks.

A few minutes later, the pre-launch checks were completed, and a warning alarm sounded throughout the ship. Tommy, Robert, and the rest of the crew left the missile launch area and the Tomahawk was lifted by machines to an upright position. A pair of sliding doors opened in the ceiling, and the missile was raised slightly above the deck and pointed towards the target, over 100 miles away. From a safe distance, the men watched as the countdown ended and the long missile lifted into the air in a cloud of smoke and fire and disappeared into the sky. A thin trail of vapor was all that was left.

Amid the cheers and celebration around him, Robert felt satisfied that he had done his job well and that everything had gone according to plan. But he couldn't help wondering about the people on that Iraqi Air Base. It was 3AM, and many of the pilots, crewman, and officers were probably sleeping in their beds. They had no idea that, in less than a minute, a massive bomb would be dropped on their heads and that many of them would die. If the missile guidance software worked well, as Tommy was sure it would, then in a matter of seconds he will have contributed to the deaths of dozens of strangers and the destructions of millions of dollars' worth of equipment.

This is war, Tommy had to remind himself, *and people die in war*. He felt Robert slap him on the back, and he let himself smile a little. Yeah, they had done a good job. But deep in his heart, Tommy wondered how many more missiles he would have to fire before it would all be over. The Gulf War had officially begun.

Can you imagine what it was like to be a soldier during the Gulf War? All four main branches of the United States military (the Air Force, the Army, the Marines, and the Navy) participated in the fighting, working together towards a common purpose with soldiers and support from some 39 other counties. Beginning on January 17, 1991 and lasting until February 28 of the same year, the Gulf War was the first significant war fought by the United States since the Vietnam War. Have you ever heard anyone talk about the Gulf war? Do you know anyone who fought in it?

In this handbook, we will learn more about this important war. We will start by learning more about what led up to it. You will see how the aggressive actions of Iraqi President Saddam Hussein led to direct involvement by the world community and its armies. We will also see how important the United Nations was during the whole process.

The next section will talk about why the Gulf War was fought. In other words, we will learn why Saddam Hussein became so aggressive and why the other countries felt that he had to be stopped. Then we will see more of what happened once the war started. From its beginning, the Gulf War was different than the other wars that had come before it. There were new technologies, new tactics, and different goals. And because the United States was working together with so many other countries, they had to be sure that their actions were supported by the whole group.

Then we will look at what it was like to be a kid back then. Whether you were living in the United States and were watching the war on TV or you were a kid in Iraq listening to the bomb explosions and gunshots, you would have had a lot of questions. You would have been scared, and adults would not have always had the answers. We will see what it was like to be a kid during those important months of the war.

Then we will see how the Gulf War ended. Although the fighting only lasted about six weeks once the United States and their allies (together called the "Coalition") got involved, it wasn't easy to bring the fighting to an end. And once the last bullet was fired, we will see a little bit of what happened afterwards. Did you know that the way the Gulf War ended led directly to the 2003 Invasion of Iraq some 12 years later? We will see how a little later on.

The Gulf War may have ended over twenty years ago, but that does not mean that it is not important for you to learn more about it. What happened during that war changed a lot about the politics and the economy of the Middle East and led to a second war that just ended a little while ago. The soldiers who fought in the Gulf War are still alive today and still think almost every day about the battles that they took part in. So are you ready to learn more about the Gulf War? Then let's begin!

Chapter 1: What Led Up to the Gulf War?

The Gulf War was fought principally between the United States and its Coalition allies against the nation of Iraq and a few of its allies. How did the fighting start? To find the answer, we have to go back in time a few years to the Iran-Iraq war, fought from 1980 to 1988. During this war, over 500,000 people died, and lots of terrible weapons were used. After a 1979 revolution in Iran, the nearby nation of Iraq was worried that Iran would become the new boss in the region. That, along with constant fighting over what the borders were between the two countries, made Saddam Hussein feel justified in invading Iran. But after his attack was stopped, Iran began to fight back, and for the next eight years both sides fought hard to win the war. Saddam had to borrow lots of money to keep the fighting going.

In 1988, a ceasefire was finally reached and the international borders set by the United Nations were accepted. However, the Iraqi government was humiliated at losing the war, had lots of debt, and the Iraqi people weren't happy. These factors (as we will see in the next section) made Saddam Hussein feel that the only option to save his country and to make it stronger would be to invade another neighboring country, this time the small country of Kuwait, to the south.

The invasion of Kuwait by the Iraqi government began on August 2, 1990. The capital of Kuwait City was bombed, and the Iraqi special forces were sent in to take over the city. At the same time, large numbers of Iraqi soldiers began to cross the border and start fighting. The Kuwaiti government had seen the large number of Iraqi soldiers but thought that they were on a spying mission- not that they were going to attack or anything. That's how it happened that, within twelve hours, most of the fighting was over.

The Iraqi soldiers destroyed many buildings in Kuwait City[16]

[16] Image source: http://lolosgossip.blogspot.com/2011/08/iraqi-invasion-of-kuwait-lets-not.html

A lot of Kuwait people suffered during the attack, and it seemed like the Iraqi soldiers were mean for no good reason; it seemed that they were being meaner than they had to be, in fact. There were reports of Iraqi soldiers beating and shooting civilians, of their chasing doctors and nurses away and leaving patients unattended in hospitals, of shooting tank rounds at buildings just to destroy them, and of using the bathroom in the main rooms of houses (instead of in the bathroom) just to be disrespectful. It seemed like there was something personal happening in Kuwait and that Iraq was being way too aggressive.

The surprise attack caught the Kuwaiti people and really the whole world totally by surprise. Within just two days, the entire country was under control of the Iraqis, and Saddam Hussein decided to appoint his cousin to be the Kuwaiti president. A few hours after the attack began Kuwait and the United States asked the United Nations to have a special meeting of the Security Council to decide what to do about Iraq's actions.

The Security Council voted on and accepted Resolution 660 the same day. In this resolution, they condemned the actions of Iraq and demanded that Iraq return to its previous position and immediately withdraw from Kuwait. Iraq paid no attention to the resolution. Four days later, Resolution 661 was passed which put economic sanctions (punishments) on Iraq for its actions of for not leaving Kuwait as they had been told to do. No nations would trade or do business with Iraq as a result of the sanctions.

On August 25, the United Nations authorized a naval blockade to enforce the economic sanctions. A line of ships would wait outside the ports of Iraq and would inspect any boats coming into or out of. If anything illegal was found, it would be confiscated.

Finally, on November 29, it was clear to the United Nations and to the whole world that Iraq was not interesting in cooperating or listening to anyone else. Although Saddam Hussein had tried to make bargains and special conditions to leave Kuwait, the United Nations was clear: Iraq had to leave right away, no ifs, ands, or buts. On that day, Resolution 678 was passed, giving Iraq until January 15, 1991, to obey the conditions of Resolution 660 (leaving Kuwait immediately).

When Iraq refused to listen to the United Nations and continued to be dangerous, the world community acted together. The United States and the coalition forces laid out a plan, and on January 17 the Operation Desert Storm began with an intensive bombing campaign against Iraq.

Chapter 2: Why Did the Gulf War Happen?

When we look back at the Gulf War, and we see how many people died and how much suffering there was, it is a perfectly normal thing to ask: "Why?" In this section, we will learn more about what motivated each side to keep on fighting. Let's start with what motivated Saddam Hussein to invade Kuwait and to refuse to withdraw his troops.

President Saddam Hussein[17]

As we saw in the previous section, after the Iran-Iraq war things weren't looking too good for Saddam Hussein or his government. He had borrowed a lot of money (about $60 billion) from Saudi Arabia and Kuwait to fight the war, and now he had to pay them back. Where would he get all of that money? Well, Iraq got most of its money from the oil that was pumped out of its many oil fields. It would refine the oil and then send it to countries around the world to be used as fuel and lubrication for machines. But there was a problem: the price of oil was getting lower and lower because Kuwait was producing more and more oil. As a result, Iraq got less money for its oil and was having trouble paying its debts.

A special organization had been formed called OPEC, and it helped to regulate how much oil was for sale at any given moment and also how much it should be sold for. Each country was told how much oil it could produce. Kuwait began to produce more than was allowed and started to make the price of oil go lower. Iraq was upset by this, saying that they were losing billions of dollars each year. But, according to Saddam Hussein, there was an even bigger problem with Kuwait: they were stealing Iraqi oil! Saddam Hussein said that the Kuwaitis were drilling sideways and putting pipes under the border and into Iraq in order to steal oil that belonged to them. As you can imagine, the Iraqi government and people were terribly upset to hear accusations like those.

[17] Image source: http://usiraq.procon.org/view.additional-resource.php?resourceID=000694

Saddam Hussein was also dealing with problems inside his own borders. After the war with Iran ended, he had a lot of unemployed soldiers with nothing to do. Foreigners who had been brought in to help the war effort soon found themselves being hated in some parts of the country by these unemployed Iraqi soldiers. Also, the Iraqi people felt that Saddam Hussein and the current government weren't good leaders; after all, they had just lost the war against Iran. Saddam was afraid that his own people would rebel against him, so he needed to find a way to get money into the country, to give his people pride in something, and to make sure that they had confidence in him as a leader. What could he do? For President Saddam Hussein, the answer was simple: invade Kuwait, take their oil, and get the nation busy again.

Saddam said that Kuwait was an illegal government that actually belonged to Iraq, and once the war started he claimed it as a 19th province of Iraq. In President Hussein's eyes, he was simply taking what already belonged to him and his people in the first place. If he wanted to blow up buildings or push them around then the world shouldn't care because it wasn't any of their business.

Well, that's where he was wrong. The world got upset over what Saddam Hussein did. But why were the United States and the Coalition forces willing to fight and, in some cases, to die? Consider some of the reasons.

First, everyone was worried about something they called the violation of Human Rights. Have you ever heard the term "human rights" before? Basically, human rights talks about how people should and should not be treated. For example, people should not be killed by their leaders, shouldn't be tortured by the enemy during a war, and should always be able to express their opinions even if they aren't popular. Well, during the Iraqi invasion of Kuwait, none of those rights were being respected.

There were even people who went before the U.S. government to talk about the brutality of the Iraqi military during the Kuwait invasion, and they told stories of how the soldiers stole medical equipment and left babies on the floor to die. Years later, it was learned that these stories weren't true at all, but stories (called "propaganda") that were meant to make the people get involved and do something. The tactic worked, and the majority of Americans got behind the war effort.

More than that, once Saddam Hussein moved into Kuwait, he was close enough to attack Saudi Arabia, one of the largest producers of oil in the world. After already having attacked one of the people he owed money to (Kuwait), many in the Coalition thought that he would now go even further and attack the other one (Saudi Arabia). The scary thing was that Iraq had plenty of soldiers and that the soldiers were ready to fight. They were experienced, eager, and willing to sacrifice everything for their country.

Finally, the Coalition was also worried about something called Weapons of Mass Destruction. Have you ever heard that term before? It is used to describe weapons that hurt a lot of people all at once. Unlike bullets (which only go where you aim them) and smart bombs (which only target specific areas) Weapons of Mass Destruction hurt everyone within a certain area, often doing so in painful ways. During the war with Iran, Iraq had used various nerve gases to kill thousands of people at one time.

Iranian soldiers wore extensive protection against nerve gas during their war with Iraq[18]

Even though weapons like that are illegal and dangerous (they go wherever the wind blows them and hurt anyone in the way), Iraq insisted on using them before, and the Coalition was afraid that they would be used again against Kuwait, Saudi Arabia, and anyone else who Iraq got angry with.

With so many factors involved, the United States and the Coalition did not feel like they could just sit around and do nothing. They thought that they had to get involved. So after Resolution 678 was passed and Iraq did not leave by the January 15 deadline, they thought that they had good reason to begin Operation Desert Storm and to begin bombing Iraq.

---

[18] Image source: http://upload.wikimedia.org/wikipedia/commons/4/49/Iranian_soldiers_in_PPE.jpg

Chapter 3: What Happened During the Gulf War?

The Gulf War, authorized by the United Nations' Security Council's Resolution 678, was carried out under a plan called Operation Desert Storm. Because it was to be a "limited war", or in other words a war just for one purpose, the goal would be to make sure as few Coalition soldiers got hurt as possible and that the war did not last one day longer than it had to. The one purpose of Operation Desert Storm would be to force the Iraqi army out of Kuwait and back into Iraq. What was the strategy used by the Coalition forces?

It was decided to start with a three-phase bombing campaign and then to send in the ground troops once the Iraqis were weak. All throughout the war Saddam Hussein would offer to withdraw his troops if certain conditions were met, but the international community did not want Iraq to feel like they had gained anything from their aggressive attack so everyone agreed that nothing less than an unconditional surrender would bring an end to the fighting.

On January 17, 1991, the first phase of the bombing began. As we saw in the introduction, some Tomahawk cruise missiles were launched from ships in the nearby Persian Gulf. These missiles had little computers inside that could guide them to a specific target. Along with the missiles, large bombers flew overhead and dropped tons and tons of explosives on specific targets. During the first phase of the bombing, the targets were air defenses. In other words, the Coalition had to make sure that the Iraqi soldiers wouldn't shoot down any of their planes.

The second phase of the bombing was communication and oil reserves. Because the army depended on good communication from Saddam Hussein (who didn't like his soldiers thinking for themselves and preferred to boss each one around), it was hoped that destroying the communication centers would make the Iraqi military break up and surrender more quickly.

The third phase of the bombing was to get the area ready for the ground troops. Military bases, runways, groups of soldiers: they were all targeted. The planes used GPS satellites to find and destroy their targets (including tanks) and made sure not to get lost, even when flying at night. Special stealth planes were difficult to spot and so could almost always hit their targets and get back to base without being caught.

Once the first part of Operation Desert Storm (the bombing) had taken place, it was time to move in the ground troops. Beginning in Kuwait, the ground troops focused on pushing the Iraqi soldiers back to where they came from. This push was called Operation Desert Sabre and it began on February 24, 1991. It was during this time that the Coalition troops saw some of the toughest fighting. There were land mines, trenches, and enemies who had been waiting there for months. The United States finally decided to just move forward with tanks that were modified to look and act like bulldozers. With their thick armor, the tanks were protected from the bullets of the soldiers, and with the big blades attached to the front they could push through the mines and fill in the trenches. The Iraqi soldiers who didn't escape were buried alive, and this became a major controversy after the war was over.

Within just four short days of beginning Operation Desert Sabre, the soldiers accomplished their goal. The Iraqi soldiers were running as fast as they could to get away from Kuwait City and back into Iraq. Moving down a road called Highway 80, the nonstop bombing by the United States and Coalition planes made many Iraqis abandon their vehicles on the side of the road and run into the desert. The road came to be called the Highway of Death.

A picture of the Highway of Death and the vehicles left behind by retreating Iraqi soldiers[19]

All throughout the war, Saddam Hussein had tried to get more support for his actions. He may have thought that the United States and others wouldn't get involved, but he soon found out how wrong he was. Once he saw how bad things looked for him, President Hussein began to try and get others to help him fight to stay in Kuwait, or to at least make him not look like such a bad guy.

First, he started by saying that he was fighting a *jihad*, or an Islamic holy war. He was hoping that other countries with governments that practice the Islamic faith would come to his aid. He hoped that Palestine, Saudi Arabia, Lebanon, Syria, and others would give him soldiers, weapons, and money. But he received hardly any support. In fact, some other Islamic countries (including Saudi Arabia, Egypt, and Syria) decided to join the Coalition and to fight *against* Iraq in the war.

Then, in a special effort to break up the unity, Saddam had an idea. What if he could get the sworn enemy of many Islamic countries (Israel) to fight alongside the Coalition? If Saudi Arabia, Egypt, and Syria saw that Israel was now part of the Coalition, they might leave it and stop fighting. So to get Israel to join the war he started to send lots of bombs towards Israel. The bombs did a lot of damage and killed some Israelis, but because they saw the bigger picture the nation of Israel refused to fight.

Finally, Saddam Hussein tried to make peace but on his own terms. He promised to leave Kuwait and to go home if everyone everywhere agreed to send all their soldiers home. For example, he wanted Israel to leave Palestine alone and for Syria to leave Lebanon. But the world community would accept anything less than a total surrender, and so the war continued.

As the Iraqi troops withdrew from Syria, they did something nasty: they set fire to all of the oil wells that they came across. By doing this, they had done this because of the landmines and dangerous conditions in the area, it would be months before some of them were put out. In the meantime, millions of barrels of oil were lost, and lots of pollution was created.

737 oil wells were set on fire when Iraq withdrew from Kuwait[20]

The United States also cared for all of the victims of the war. They brought in food for the Kuwaiti refugees and took care of the civilians injured by the fighting. The Coalition was doing well, and Operation Desert Storm was having considerable success in its mission. The Iraqi soldiers were on the run, and it looked like the Gulf War would soon be coming to its end.

---

[20] Image source: http://www.army.mil/media/231324/

Chapter 4: What Was It Like to Be a Kid Back Then?

Have you ever wondered what it would have been like to have been a kid in Iraq during Operation Desert Storm? One Iranian kid was named Amir M. Emadi. Because of the Iranian Revolution that led to the Iran-Iraq war, he and his family ran away to Iraq looking for a safe place to live. In a place called Camp Ashraf, he waited along with his family member as the Coalition bombed Iraq. What do you think he felt like? All grown up now, Amir explains what it felt like to listen to the bombs fall all around him:

> "Looking back, it seems so long ago because I was just a child, but I recall the trauma. We were in the middle of a war, not of our own choosing. The United States had just started to attack Iraq following the Iraqi invasion of Kuwait. We had no water, no medicine, no school, no life. There was no electricity. We had to live in bunkers, sometimes 30 or 40 kids in one place. The huge bombs, which I later learned were 1,000-pound JDMs, shook the earth around us every night and day. It was horrific. To me, it was Nagasaki. To me, it was Katrina."[21]

Can you imagine how scared Amir and his family were? You see, although there were lots of smart bombs used to hit specific targets, there were also lots of normal bombs dropped, the kind that explode on whatever they happen to hit. That means that lots of kids (like Amir, who is in the picture below) had to worry about a bomb being dropped on their house even though they weren't fighting in the war.

Amir M. Emadi was a refugee with his family in Iraq during the bombing of Operation Desert Storm[22]

As a kid, Amir didn't understand everything about the war. He didn't know why planes were flying overhead and dropping bombs on his neighbors, and he didn't know why far away ships that he couldn't even see were shooting missiles at him. His parents weren't soldiers either, and yet all of them were afraid every single day that the next bomb might fall on it too close to them.

Kids like Amir probably heard the adults talk about Kuwait and President Hussein and oil, but do you think he would have understood everything? Really, in the middle of so much violence, most kids (and adults) just want things to calm down and be like they were before. So you can imagine that if you were a kid living in Kuwait or Iraq during the Gulf War, you would just be hoping that each bomb dropped would be the last.

But what would it have been like to have lived in the United States during the Gulf War? Well, over almost 700,000 Americans were sent to fight the war, so that means that there were a lot of families whose fathers and brothers and sons went off, and some of them never came back. How would you have felt having to say goodbye to your dad as he goes off to fight? Would you have been sad? Do you think you would have understood why it was important for him to go and fight that war?

The Gulf War was different than other wars because of the type of news coverage that it received. Instead of waiting hours or even days to find out what was going on, there were reporters connected to satellites that gave instant news of bombs being dropped, attacks, and overall progress of the operation. In fact, some people even called it "The Video Game War" because it was happening live on people's TVs just like a video game. But how would you have felt watching those news reports and knowing that your dad or your big brother was in the middle of all the fighting? Would you have been worried?

Two brothers, one of whom served the Gulf War[23]

Kids at home in the United States had to worry a lot about their family members who were fighting in the war. As you can imagine, when some soldiers didn't come home from the fighting there were a lot of sad families.

The Gulf War, for the first time, let people of the other side of the world feel like they were in the middle of the fighting. While it gave everyone more information, it also meant more worry, more tension, and http://www.newyorkwidesidewalk.com/and-backohen couldn't avoid getting caught up in it all.

Chapter 5: How Did the Gulf War End?

As we saw, Operation Desert Storm focused first on an intensive three-phase bombing campaign and then on a quick moving ground assault. Within four days of beginning the ground assault, the Coalition had so much success and had pushed the Iraqi military back to quickly that U.S. President George H.W. Bush ordered a ceasefire on February 28.

As we saw earlier, the Iraqis had no made a quiet retreat. Not only did they keep fighting along the way but they also set fire to all of the Kuwait oil wells as they passed them. But why would they do such a thing? Destroying land during a retreat is a common wartime tactic called a "scorched earth policy". The idea is not to leave anything that might be useful to the enemy. The soldiers usually take food, stop up water wells, burn crops, and destroy houses. It was this tactic that helped the Russians to fight well against the German Nazis during World War Two.

The retreating Iraqi army wanted to set fire to the oil wells so that neither the Americans nor anyone else could use the oil for money or fuel. What's worse, the whole area was so surrounded by mines that the oil fires couldn't be put out right away, some of them burning all the way until November.

But after the Iraqi military had been beaten so badly and were retreating back into Iraq, Saddam Hussein realized that he could not win. The American troops had undone all of his hard work in only four days, and they had advanced across the border and into Iraq. A ceasefire had been called, but Saddam Hussein would have to agree to certain terms before there could be peace. What were the terms?

As you remember, there were several reasons that the United States and the Coalition decided to go to war against Iraq. They were worried about Iraq's treatment of Kuwait, and they were also worried about the dangerous weapons that Iraq had used during wars. They wanted to make sure that these Weapons of Mass Destruction (which are illegal to use according to the Geneva Convention) would never be put to use again. The terms that Saddam Hussein had to agree to end the war addressed both of those.

First, President Hussein had to acknowledge that Kuwait was an independent and sovereign state and not to try to invade it and claim it for Iraq again. Saddam Hussein did so and, in fact, shortly before he died, he apologized to the people of Kuwait for having invaded and admitting that it was the wrong thing to do.

The second condition had to do with the Weapons of Mass Destruction that the government of Iraq had. The country would have to allow United Nations inspectors to come visit them and help them to dispose of the weapons and to inspect and make sure that there weren't any more hidden away.

Saddam Hussein accepted both major conditions and the ceasefire became official. In addition, the economic sanctions and the naval blockade against Iraq were lifted (Cancelled). During the next month preparations were made and on March 11, 1991, American and Coalition troops began to leave Iraq and Kuwait.

Chapter 6: What Happened After the Gulf War?

After the Gulf War ended, everyone was happy that the fighting had finally stopped. There were no more Tomahawk missiles flying through the air, and there were no more families separated by the war. Kuwait and Iraq began to rebuild their countries after all of the fighting and the Coalition forces went home to their families. But the war left some massive holes in the world, and some fires were started that would keep burning for a long time.

First off, look at some of the statistics. Over 350, Americans died during the war. Whether it was from bullets or bombs, each one of those deaths meant someone had lost a dad, a mom, a brother, a sister, or a friend. Fellow soldiers cried for the ones who they had lost, and America watched on TV as the bodies were brought home and the families cried on camera.

Soldiers bring out coffins of Americans who died during the Gulf War[24]

But America wasn't the only country to cry for dead soldiers. Iraq lost some 3,500 civilians and over 20,000 soldiers. Nine of the Coalition countries lost at least one soldier each, and many lost more than one. But many more deaths occurred after the ceasefire because of conditions created by the war.

Although the Coalition did not remove Saddam Hussein from power, they did secretly that his own people would rise up against him and do so. In fact, some members of the United States government had even told different groups inside of Iraq that they would have U.S. support if they ever tried to change the president for someone less aggressive. Counting on that support, Kurdish people in the North and Shiite Muslims in the South of Iraq tried to fight against Saddam but were not successful. You see, the United States didn't help them like the people had hoped, and so Saddam ended up being violent with some of them and killing many thousands of rebels. He was a particularly cruel dictator when it came to dealing with his own people.

Veterans of the Gulf War who returned home were happy to be alive and happy that they never had to deal with Weapons of Mass Destruction like during the Iran-Iraq War. But as the years went by, they began to notice that they weren't feeling quite right and that some of their children were born with problems. Their symptoms aren't yet entirely understood, but it has become clear to many people that the veterans of Operation Desert Storm were exposed to something dangerous while fighting the war and that some of them are getting sick.

Of the almost 700,000 Americans sent to fight in the Gulf War, about 250,000 of them share many of the same symptoms. Called "Gulf War Syndrome", the symptoms may be as mild as constant tiredness to more serious like ones like life-threatening tumors. While no one can be one hundred percent sure of the causes, it seems like some of the pills given to the soldiers to protect them from nerve gas, and the smoke from all the burning oil wells have both had terrible long-term effects on their bodies.

Another effect of the Gulf War that reaches down through the years has to do with one of the conditions that Saddam Hussein had to accept to end the war. Do you remember how everyone was worried that Saddam Hussein would use some of those nasty Weapons of Mass Destruction again like he had before? Do you remember one of the conditions that he had to agree to in order to end the war? That's right: he had to promise to allow United Nations inspectors into his country to make sure he was disposing of all illegal weapons (like nerve gas, mustard gas, and cyanide bombs) and to make sure that he wasn't making any new ones.

Saddam Hussein didn't like the arrangement one bit, but he accepted it in order to stop the Americans from bombing his country any more. But why do you think that Saddam Hussein had a problem with U.N. inspectors coming into his country to check for weapons? Well, how do you feel when your parents come into your room to see whether or not you have done your chores? Don't you feel like it is an invasion of your privacy? And what if they went through your drawers and checked your phone to make sure that you weren't doing anything bad? How would you feel?

Saddam Hussein quickly started to have problems with the inspectors. It wasn't long after the war when he began to give them trouble, and eventually he stopped allowing them to come into his land. Remember, this was the same man who invaded a country because he thought they were stealing his oil; so imagine how much he would hate anyone else making him look like an immature little kid.

The fact that he didn't let inspectors come into his country made a lot of people scared and upset. Not only was he violating the terms of the ceasefire but he was also making a lot of people think that he was up to no good. It's kind of like when a kid doesn't want his teachers looking in his locker because he knows that something bad is in there. A lot of important leaders around the world, especially in the United States and Great Britain, became convinced that Saddam Hussein was making more Weapons of Mass Destruction and that it wouldn't be long before he used them again against an innocent population.

In November 2002, U.S. President George W. Bush went before the United Nations Security Council and explained his concerns about Iraq. The Security Council agreed with him and issued Resolution 1441 which gave Iraq "a final opportunity to comply with its disarmament obligations" that it had been ordered to do by previous resolutions. A unanimous vote approved the resolution and Iraq said that it would comply. However, further problems between Saddam Hussein and U.N. inspectors led the United

States and Great Britain (this time without United Nations support) to invade Iraq again on March 20, 2003, thus beginning the Iraq War.

The effects of the Gulf War went far beyond the immediate days and months after the ceasefire: they shaped the world for the next twenty years and continued to lead to more deaths and eventually to the execution of Saddam Hussein by his own people in 2006.

Conclusion

Did you learn something new about the Gulf War after reading this handbook, something that maybe you didn't know before? A lot happened during those seven weeks, and a lot of brave men and women fought to stop a terrible man. Some of them paid with the ultimate price: their lives. Have you ever spoken to anyone who fought in the Gulf War? While not everyone is willing to talk about the things that they saw and did while in the war, try to see what you can find out from them and what lessons they learned from their time in the Middle East.

In the meantime, let's review some of the important things that we learned in this handbook. We started by learning more about what led up to it. Do you remember what some of the things were that happened just before the war started? Well, remember that Iraq was in a pretty bad situation after their war with Iran and that President Hussein was looking for a way to make his people respect him again. He thought that a bold attack (like invading Kuwait) would be the thing to do. He thought that his fellow Arab countries would support him and that the United States wouldn't get involved. Obviously, he was dead wrong.

We also saw how important the United Nations and its Security Council was during the whole process. From the first meeting called by Kuwait and the U.S. to the final ceasefire agreement, this international body helped to promote good communication between everyone involved.

The next section talked about why the Gulf War was fought. In other words, we learned why Saddam Hussein became so aggressive and why the other countries felt that he had to be stopped. Do you remember what the reasons were? Well, Saddam wanted to stop the Kuwaiti people from selling so much oil (some of which he thought was his) and he wanted to keep his power. The Coalition nations (including the United States) were worried about the human rights violation in Kuwait, about the oil in Saudi Arabia, and about the Weapons of Mass Destruction in Iraq. For that reason, both sides felt that they could not stop fighting and would not back down.

Then we saw more of what happened once the war started. From its beginning, the Gulf War was different than the other wars that had come before it. There were new technologies, new tactics, and different goals. We saw how "smart" bombs were used to increase the chances of only destroying military targets and not innocent civilians. There were also special tactics used to limit the amount of American casualties (deaths). In three phases, the Coalition forces bombed targets in Iraq. They began with Iraqi air defenses, then moved on to communications centers and oil reserves, and finished with military bases and individual tanks.

After the bombing had ended, the ground war began. The ground war was so effective that, within just four days, the objective had been reached: the Iraqi military had withdrawn from Kuwait and retreated back into Iraq. Although they had lit the oil wells on fire and kept shooting along the way, it was safe to say that the war was just about over. We also saw how because the United States was working together with so many other countries, they had to be sure that their actions were supported by the whole group. That was one of the reasons that they chose not to take Saddam Hussein out of power but just to hope that his own people would do it.

Then we saw what it was like to be a kid back then. Whether you were living in the United States and were watching the war on TV or you were a kid in Iraq listening to the bomb explosions and gunshots, you would have had a lot of questions. You would have been scared, and adults would not have always had the answers. We saw real life examples of kids who said goodbye to family members that went to fight in the Gulf War and of others who had to hide from the bombs that were being dropped on their towns. It was a scary and sad time to be a kid.

We also saw how the Gulf War ended. Although the fighting only lasted about six weeks once the United States and their allies (together called the "Coalition") got involved, it wasn't easy to bring the fighting to an end. The Iraqi military was large, was experienced, and had lots of time to prepare their positions before the fighting started. Sometimes the Americans had to do strange and controversial things to win, like the time they used tanks with blades like bulldozers to bury enemy Iraqis in their trenches.

Once Saddam Hussein saw that the fighting was too much for him, and his men, he agreed to the conditions set out by the United Nations and surrendered. Do you remember what the two main conditions were? That's right: he had to acknowledge that Kuwait was an independent country and not part of Iraq, and he also had to allow United Nations inspectors to come into Iraq and make sure there were no Weapons of Mass Destruction that might be used in a future battle.

And once the last bullet was fired, we finally saw e a little bit of what happened afterwards. We saw some of the fighting within Iraq after the Coalition forces left and how a lot of people were killed by Saddam Hussein and his government. And did you see how the Gulf War ended led directly to the 2003 Invasion of Iraq some 12 years later? Remember how we saw that President Hussein got tired of all the U.N. inspectors in his country and eventually told them to get lost and never come back. The world didn't like that, but even when the United Nations *ordered* Saddam to let the inspectors back in, he didn't obey. Finally, the United States and Great Britain, convinced that something bad was going on in Iraq, didn't wait for U.N. permission and went ahead and invaded Iraq. It was during this war that Saddam Hussein was executed by his own people.

The Gulf War forever changed the politics of the Middle East and of the world. It showed how much good the governments can accomplish when they get together and talk but also how much harm can be caused by just one man with too much power. What was your favorite part of this handbook?

Even though we saw how some sad things happened during the Gulf War, we can be happy that the Kuwaiti people knew that they could ask for help from the international community and get it. Today, we don't know what will happen in the future. Iraq is different than it was when under Saddam Hussein and has become a friend of the United States. But in the future if another little country is attacked by a big one, do think that the world will listen? Will they support the innocent and fight against the bad guys? The Gulf War showed us that it can be done if everyone works together.

A special parade held for veterans of the Gulf War after they came home victorious[25]

---

[25] Image source: http://www.pri.org/theworld/?q=node/21590

The War in Afganistan
A History Just for Kids

Soldiers fight against Taliban soldiers in Afghanistan[26]

---

[26] Image source: http://rootsaction.org/

Introduction

Sergeant Mikey Hooper has never experienced heat like this before. Everything is wet and sticky: his socks, his undershirt, and even his underwear. The 115 degree weather makes him feel like he is inside of an oven, and the pack that he has to carry weighs over 80 pounds. Between the heat and the weight of his equipment (including the body armor that he wears under his vest) Mikey feels like he is moving in slow motion whenever he marches with his squad on patrol or when he is running towards an enemy's position. Basic training back in South Carolina had been intense, and at the time Mikey had thought that the Drill Instructors were just being mean by making the men run so much in the heat and go long periods without food and sleep. But now that he was here in Afghanistan, Mikey saw that the boot camp was meant to prepare him for the life of a Marine.

Sometimes he was woken up during the night by explosions, and sometimes he felt that he didn't always have enough water out here in the hot desert. When the combat finally started, though, he wasn't normally too scared. His months of experience had taught him to just stay focused on making sure that his men carried out their mission safely. Sometimes they had to protect Afghan civilians from the Taliban fighters; sometimes they had to enter caves and villages looking for the bad guys; sometimes they had to defend their fellow American and British soldiers from the attacks of Al-Qaeda fighters.

Today, Mikey and his men were in the mountains that lie to the east of the Afghan capital of Kabul. The area that they were walking in had been hit previously by American bombs, and now the soldiers were moving in, looking through the rubble and collapsed buildings for members of the Al-Qaeda terrorist organization, which was supported by the local Taliban government. As they walked between two high, rock hills, and around a bend in the road that led to the village, Mikey suddenly heard a distant *pop* and felt a pain that he could only describe as if somebody had punched him in the chest. He fell onto his back and used what little breath he had to warn his men about the attack.

A strong pair of hands grabbed him by the shoulders and pulled him back around the corner, behind the rocks that seemed to be exploding around him. The medic came running to look at him, but after catching his breath Mikey said "It hit my armor…I'm okay. Is anyone else hit?"

No one else was. Mikey had narrowly avoided getting killed by an Al-Qaeda sniper. The shots kept ringing out and echoing through the narrow canyon, and all the dust was making it hard to see what was going on. Mikey told his Corporal, John Eckard, to radio for an airstrike. While he did so, Mikey sat up and felt the blood rush to his head. With the help of the medic, he got to his feet and made a plan: they had to keep the Al-Qaeda fighters busy so that they wouldn't run away before the airstrike came in.

It was decided that they would split into two groups. One would stay back and provide cover fire while Mikey and the other half moved forward and engaged the enemy. Within thirty seconds, the plan was underway. While the men in the back fired small bursts of fire with their guns, Mikey and his men moved in pairs around the corner and behind some large rocks twenty yards ahead. The canyon was alive with the sounds of yelling and small explosions. It seemed like the enemy didn't have any grenades or rockets, which was a good thing for Mikey and his men; they wouldn't have been able to escape the explosion of shrapnel. Even so, those bullets were still plenty scary when they came flying towards your head.

For ten minutes, the fighting got more and more intense. Mikey could hardly stick his helmet out from around the rock without pieces of it exploding in his face from all the enemy bullets. Finally, a message came over the radio that the plane was on its way. The Navy had sent two F/A-18 Hornets from a carrier stationed in the North Arabian Sea. The pilots of the jets had requested that a smoke grenade be thrown to mark the men's position. Mikey gave the order and a grenade was thrown that signaled their position. Mikey grabbed the radio and said: "The target is east of the orange smoke, I repeat: east of the orange smoke." He clicked off the radio and yelled "Bombs away!"

His men all dropped to the ground and yelled "Bombs away!" The enemy must have figured out that something was happening when they saw the smoke because the bullets stopped flying and Mikey could just make out the shapes of men running away through the smoke and dust. Mikey assumed they were going to try to retreat to the other side of the hills, but it was too late for that. Mikey and his men had succeeded in giving the Navy boys perfect targets, a group of sitting ducks. The Marines never saw the jets; they just heard them for a split second before two massive explosions shook the entire canyon. By the time the smoke and dust had cleared, it was clear that there was no one left to fire at them.

Even so, Mikey and his moved carefully towards the enemy's position seventy yards away. They found a mess of dead bodies. No one laughed or joked. They weren't happy to have helped to kill these men. But, these men were terrorists who wanted to hurt innocent people. They had refused to stop being violent, so they had to be stopped. It was that simple.

Mikey grabbed the radio from the soldier who carried it. "This is Sergeant Hooper confirming 16 hostiles down, no casualties among my men." The voice on the other end congratulated him for completing his mission without losing a single man. Mikey said thanks and sat down with his back against the rocky wall. Taking a drink of water, he felt himself getting dizzy, forgetting that just a few minutes earlier he had been shot in the chest. The medic saw him and recommended that they head back to base so that Mikey could get checked out.

Mikey smiled. *Base.* It made it sound like they were a bunch of kids out here playing hide-and-seek. He agreed with the medic, gave the order to move out, and headed back with his men towards the camp. Tomorrow would be another day, with another mission, and another tough decision to make. But none of that mattered right now. He had survived this battle; he had survived another day in Afghanistan.

Does it sound like it would be exciting to fight alongside the brave Marines in Afghanistan? While sometimes it sounds like something out of a movie, the reality of war is different. There aren't actually a lot of heroes like the ones we see in theaters; more than anything you see teams of people working together and just trying to survive another day. The soldiers who kill their enemies aren't always happy about what they've done; they just see it as something that they have been told to do by their superiors, and they carry out the job. Even though it isn't quite over yet, the War in Afghanistan has had a big impact in the world. Do you know anyone who was involved in that war or who has an opinion about it?

In this book, we will learn a lot about the War in Afghanistan. The first section will tell us more about what led up to it. We will look a little at the history of Afghanistan to find out how such bad guys like the Taliban could ever become the ruling party in the country. We will also see a little of what life was like when the Taliban was in charge.

Then, in the next section, we will see why the war actually happened. Although things had been bad in Afghanistan for a while, why did the United Nations decide to get involved in 2001? The answer had a lot to do with the terrorist attack of September 11, 2001, and with a lot of strong emotions. We will also see in this section that some people think that the war was and still is illegal, and that no one should have fought it.

Then, we will see some of the interesting details of how the war was fought. The beginning was pretty standard, but the final part has been difficult and the NATO (North Atlantic Treaty Organization) troops are still having a tough time doing their job and keeping the region stable and safe. Along with the bravery of the NATO troops, we will also see how many Afghan men and women have been affected by the war and how they have helped to fight against the bad guys.

The section after that will show us what it would be like to be a kid living in Afghanistan during the war. Daily life was changed in many ways from before the war; sometimes in a good way and sometimes in a bad way. Then, the next sections will talk about how the war started to wind down and what significant changes Afghanistan has seen since it started.

Are you ready to learn more about this war? As we do so, try to keep an eye out for how the religion of the Taliban and Al-Qaeda fighters has affected their actions and the way that they deal with outside nations. Whether or not anyone meant for it to, religion became a central factor in this war and continues to be so in everything that happens in Afghanistan today. So buckle up, and let's move on to the next section!

Chapter 1: What Led Up to the War in Afghanistan?

Afghanistan is a country with a rich history[27]

The country that we now know as Afghanistan used to be under the influence of the British Empire. For several decades, the Afghan people had to listen to the British and make decisions that would make them happy. Eventually, the Afghan people became independent of the British, and some of their leaders tried hard to make their country a better place. But no matter how hard they tried, those leaders could never make everyone happy at the same time. No matter who was in charge, it seemed like someone else had a better idea of how to do things and how the Afghan people should live their lives. This led to a lot of violence throughout the years, and even some periods of absolute civil war.

During World War Two and the Cold War, Afghanistan stayed neutral, which means that they didn't take one side or the other. They decided to just worry about their own problems and not those of other countries. But in 1978, Afghan people who liked the Communist way of doing things overthrew the local government to try and make a government like the one that the U.S.S.R. (the Soviets) had.

As you can imagine, not everyone was happy about it. Those who didn't like Communism started to fight back and thus a civil war began. The Soviets got involved to help their fellow party members and soon there were Soviet soldiers marching in the streets and mountaintops of Afghanistan as part of the war also. The United States thought that the Soviets were trying to spread their influence and started to get scared and for a while it looked like the U.S. might even get involved in the fighting too. Although they didn't send any soldiers, they did send money and weapons to help the anti-communist fighters, and it wasn't until 1989 when the Soviets finally left.

From 1989 to 1992, the anti-communist fighters (called the Mujahedeen) who had fought against the Soviets now turned their attention to the Afghan Communists. The Mujahedeen were supported by the U.S., and they were finally able to overthrow the Communist government in 1992, after three years of fighting. In case you are counting, you are probably starting to realize that since at least 1978 this area has had one war after another for many years. The one that started in 1978 when the Communists took over was called the Saur Revolution, and marked the time when the common people started to fight against the government.

As we saw, in 1992, the Communist government was overthrown, and on April 24 the different political groups got together to decide how to run the country now that the Communists weren't in charge anymore. They formed something called the "Peshawar Accord". All of the groups (but one) agreed to form a new country called The Islamic State of Afghanistan. They thought that they had found a new way to run the country without outside interference and without fighting anymore. However, one political party, named Hezbi Islami, did not agree. With help from Pakistan, they began to attack their fellow Afghanis and to try to prevent any efforts at peace and unity.

Some other nearby countries liked what was going on in Afghanistan and so didn't try to stop the fighting. They thought that if Afghanistan fell apart then they could take over the land and make their own countries stronger. So Saudi Arabia and Iran each supported other groups within the Afghan government, playing them like chess pieces, hoping that eventually the country would be too weak to defend itself and that an outside country could just move in and become the new boss.

As you can imagine, it wasn't a great time to be living in Afghanistan. There were different groups if people fighting for control of the country and the groups all seemed to be hurting lots of people and getting away with it. There was the main government in the capital that was under attack by Hezbi Islami, and then other parts of the country were under control of local militias (small armies) who got their money from foreign countries. Many of the common people felt like no one was looking out for them and that no one had their interests in mind. Thousands of Afghanis had run away to other countries, and those who stayed sometimes had to worry about being attacked by the militia groups. Who would protect them?

In Pakistan, young Afghan Muslim refugees had gone to special religious schools where they were taught about a variety of subjects. Those who went to these schools would sometimes go back to their country and stick together in groups, to protect each other against the bad conditions. One young man, named Mohammed Omar, had gone to one of these schools and was tired of seeing his fellow Afghans mistreated by the militias and of seeing so many people not respecting his religion of Islam. Together with a group of about 50 friends, he formed a new political and religious group called the Taliban in his hometown of Kandahar, near the border with Pakistan.

The Taliban quickly earned the reputation of being people who enforce the laws of the Islamic holy book, the Quran. In the spring of 1994, they were reported to have freed two girls who had been kidnapped and mistreated by a local militia. They punished the people responsible, and the local citizens were happy that someone was looking out for them, someone who believed and respected the same things as they did.

Within a few months, thousands of young men joined this exciting new group, and they started to fight to take over Afghanistan and to unify it under one type of rule, a type of government that respected the religion of Islam above all else. During 1994, they took over about one-third of Afghanistan's provinces and the people living there. In early 1995, they began to attack the capital city of Kabul. But things weren't so easy, and the Taliban started to lose a lot of battles against the main government of Afghanistan.

Finally, on September 27, 1996, the Taliban moved into the capital (which the main government had abandoned so as not to be fighting in the city streets) and established themselves as the new bosses. While some people thought that the Taliban were honestly just like a big puppet for Pakistan, others were happy to see leaders who took their jobs seriously and who wanted to make the Islamic religion a part of the government and everyday life of the people.

Once they were in the capital, the Taliban wanted to make sure they were in control in the whole country. To do so, they used violence. During the next few years, from 1996 to 2001, reports started to come out of mean things done to people who broke the laws of the Taliban or who refused to support them. Some people were beat, and others were even killed. We will see more in a future section about some of the bad things that the Taliban is accused of having done.

The Taliban, along with treating its own people harshly, also started to get a bad reputation because of the friends that they had; in particular, for having connections with Al-Qaeda, a terrorist organization founded by Osama Bin Laden. This friendship would soon make the enemies of Al-Qaeda the enemies of Afghanistan.

Chapter 2: Why Did the War in Afghanistan Happen?

As we have seen, things in Afghanistan weren't going terrifically well. The Afghan people hadn't had a stable government for a long time, and the people who were in charge weren't always the nicest guys. The country was finally taken over by a new religious and political group called the Taliban, but they seemed to do as much bad stuff as they did good stuff. So you might wonder why anyone from another country would get involved. The Afghan people might not react well to a foreign government marching in, and the Taliban certainly would not be happy about it. So why did the United States (together with several other countries) lead an invasion into this country?

The world knew what was happening in Afghanistan, but it seemed more like something that Afghanistan itself and their neighbors should be worried about. Why should the United States and other Western countries worry about what was happening on the other side of the globe?

All of that changed on September 11, 2001.

The World Trade Center burns after the September 11, 2001 terrorist attack[28]

Do you remember hearing about the terrorist attacks of September 11, 2001? Four planes from the east coast were stolen by a group of nineteen terrorists. They hijacked the planes once they were in the air and made the planes fly in a different direction. Two of them were flown into the World Trade Centers; one was flown into the Pentagon building in Washington D.C.; and one crashed in Pennsylvania, perhaps on its way to Washington D.C.

The United States and honestly the whole world were stunned and absolutely surprised by the attacks. Although it was not the first time that terrorists had attacked the United States, or even the World Trade Center itself, it was the first time that anyone had been so successful and that so many people had died. 2,977 people were killed in the attacks, plus the 19 hijackers. Others died later on because of sickness or injuries received during the rescue attempts.

[28] Image source: http://commons.wikimedia.org/

The world watched on live TV as the buildings fell, as desperate people trapped in the burning towers jumped to their deaths, and as firefighters tried their best to save the victims. Americans were glued to their TVs for hours and cried as they saw the horrible scenes happen live and then again as they were replayed over and over again. Even for people living in faraway California and Hawaii, it felt like the terrorists were in their backyard.

The American people had been hit hard by terrorism, and lots of families had suffered for it. The American people wanted revenge. They wanted to find the people responsible and to make them pay. Even though the hijackers themselves were dead, they wanted to find the people that had taught, trained, and sent the hijackers on this mission of death. But how could they ever identify the hijackers? Like an exciting movie, the clues started to come together in the hours and days following the attacks. Within 72 hours, all of the hijackers had been identified. How?

Knowing that they were going to die during the attacks, the hijackers left behind a lot of clues and did not try to hide who they were. They bought their tickets with their credit cards, used their real names when making the room reservations, and left clues in hotel rooms and parked cars that were soon discovered. It was learned that the 19 attackers were religious fanatics from the Islam religion. Do you know what a fanatic is? A religious fanatic is someone who goes to extremes for their faith and is willing to hurt other people if they don't have the same religion as them. These men were Islamic fanatics and believed that the attacks were a part of a *jihad*, or holy Islamic war.

Can you believe that? The men who killed so many innocent victims, including kids, thought that God would reward them for their actions. But who trained and prepared these 19 fanatics to do this terrible thing, to carry out the attacks of September 11th? It was learned that all 19 of the men were members of an organization called Al-Qaeda, a terrorist group started by a man named Osama Bin Laden.

Now the American people wanted to find Osama Bin Laden and rest of his Al-Qaeda group and make them pay for what they had done. On September 18, 2001, a special law was passed that gave the President permission to use military authority in order to find and stop the terrorists responsible for the attacks. But where was Al-Qaeda hiding? It was learned that they were in camps and caves spread across Afghanistan.

How did the President of the United States, George W. Bush, think that Americans could get a hold of those terrorists living so far away? In a statement to Congress on September 20, 2001, he made the position of the United States clear, and he also made a demand of the Taliban government in Afghanistan. During that speech, he said important some pretty important things about Al-Qaeda and their relationship to the Taliban. For example, look at the quote below:

> "The leadership of al Qaeda has great influence in Afghanistan and supports the Taliban regime in controlling most of that country. In Afghanistan, we see al Qaeda's vision for the world. Afghanistan's people have been brutalized -- many are starving, and many have fled. Women are not allowed to attend school. You can be jailed for owning a television. Religion can be practiced only as their leaders dictate. A man can be jailed in Afghanistan if his beard is not long enough.
>
> The United States respects the people of Afghanistan -- after all, we are currently its largest source of humanitarian aid -- but we condemn the Taliban regime. It is not only repressing its own people, it is threatening people everywhere by sponsoring and sheltering and supplying terrorists. By aiding and abetting murder, the Taliban regime is committing murder."[29]

During this speech, given just nine days after the attacks of September 11th, President Bush makes it clear that the Taliban is best friends with Al-Qaeda and that the Taliban is a dangerous government guilty of doing some awful things to its people. In his speech, President Bush continued:

> "And tonight, the United States of America makes the following demands on the Taliban: Deliver to United States authorities all the leaders of al Qaeda who hide in your land. Release all foreign nationals, including American citizens, you have unjustly imprisoned. Protect foreign journalists, diplomats and aid workers in your country. Close immediately and permanently every terrorist training camp in Afghanistan, and hand over every terrorist, and every person in their support structure, to appropriate authorities. Give the United States full access to terrorist training camps, so we can make sure they are no longer operating. Our enemy is a radical network of terrorists, and every government that supports them. These demands are not open to negotiation or discussion. The Taliban must act, and act immediately. They will hand over the terrorists, or they will share in their fate. From this day forward, any nation that continues to harbor or support terrorism will be regarded by the United States as a hostile regime."[30]

President Bush during his September 20, 2001 speech to Congress[31]

Do you understand how important those words were? President Bush was essentially telling the Taliban that if they didn't hand over Al-Qaeda and shut down the camps, then the United States was going to fight against them the same as they were fighting against Al-Qaeda! The American people wanted to stop the terrorists responsible for the 9/11 attacks, and this was the best way that they knew how.

Along with the fact that the Taliban was protecting the Al-Qaeda terrorists, President Bush also mentioned how bad life was under the Taliban rule. He mentioned how severe punishments were given for something like not having a long beard or for owning a television. So the United States and other countries were also worried about the human rights abuses happening in the country. Do you know what "human rights" means? It means the right that all people have to a certain amount of freedom and to not have to worry about certain things. For example, no one should have to worry about whether the government will hurt them, whether the police will do the right thing, or whether they will have enough food to eat; those are basic human rights. However, in Afghanistan, when the Taliban was in charge, not everyone had those rights. Some people were mistreated by the police, others didn't have enough food, and others weren't even allowed to leave the house.

Women, especially, were not given a lot of freedom under Taliban rule; a lot of girls weren't allowed to go to school or even to leave the house unless they were accompanied by a man. Would you like to have lived in a country like that?

So how did the Taliban respond to President Bush's demand that they hand over the leaders of Al-Qaeda? The Taliban did not want to cooperate with the United States. Not only did it view them as a foreign power that shouldn't be pushing them around but it also thought that because the American government wasn't organized according to the teachings of Islam that it wouldn't handle the situation properly. So, the Taliban refused to turn over Al-Qaeda and Osama Bin laden and instead suggested on October 5, 2001 that if the U.S. could provide enough proof then the Taliban would try Bin Laden in an Afghan court.

That answer wasn't good enough for President Bush. On October 7, 2001, United States Special Forces entered the country and at the same time the bombing of the capital started. The War in Afghanistan had begun.

Chapter 3: What Happened During the War in Afghanistan?

When the United States invaded Afghanistan on October 7, 2001 in an operation called "Operation Enduring Freedom. The operation had two main goals:

- find and capture all members of Al-Qaeda and bring them to justice
- put an end to and replace the Taliban regime that mistreated the Afghan people

In order to meet these goals, it was decided to start with a bombing campaign like normal but also to quickly move in troops to start taking over the villages and provinces of Afghanistan. The bombing began that same day as the invasion and made it easier for troops to take over important military positions. Planes from way up high in the sky dropped bombs on Al-Qaeda training camps, and Apache helicopters attacked special targets and were strong enough to not be shot down by the Taliban's anti-aircraft guns.

An Apache helicopter used by the British during the War in Afghanistan[32]

Something else that President Bush said during his speech on September 20 made a lot of people start thinking. He said:

> "Perhaps the NATO Charter reflects best the attitude of the world: An attack on one is an attack on all. The civilized world is rallying to America's side. They understand that if this terror goes unpunished, their own cities, their own citizens may be next. Terror, unanswered, can not only bring down buildings, it can threaten the stability of legitimate governments. And you know what, we're not going to allow it."[33]

[32] Image source: http://www.graftingcorpsetimes.com/
[33] Quotation source: http://georgewbush-whitehouse.archives.gov/

In his speech, President Bush tried to explain that Americans weren't the only ones who should be worried about the activities of Al-Qaeda and the Taliban. He made it clear that an attack against one Western nation was like an attack against all of them, because they were all partners and because they all stood for the same thing. For that reason, some countries chose to help the United States with the invasion, including Great Britain, Australia, and Canada. But how did the Taliban and Al-Qaeda respond to the invasion?

Of course, the Taliban and Al-Qaeda used all of their weapons and energy to fight against the invading forces, called "The Coalition". The Taliban, because it was identified mainly by its religious beliefs and practices, felt like it was being targeted because of its faith, and not its politics. They went so far as to say that what the United States and Coalition were doing was an "attack on Islam."

In November of 2002, Osama Bin laden gave an interview where he threatened all Western nations that attacked any Islamic nation. He said:

> "What do your governments want by allying themselves with the criminal gang in the White House against Muslims? What do your governments want from their alliance with America in attacking us in Afghanistan? I mention in particular Britain, France, Italy, Canada, Germany and Australia. We warned Australia before not to join in [the war] in Afghanistan, and [against] its despicable effort to separate East Timor. It ignored the warning until it woke up to the sounds of explosions in Bali…This is unfair. It is time that we get even. You will be killed just as you kill, and will be bombed just as you bomb."[34]

Yes, both the Taliban and Al-Qaeda saw the War in Afghanistan as part of something larger. Instead of seeing it as punishment for the attacks of 9/11 or for their harsh treatment of the people of Afghanistan, they felt like they were the victims. They felt like they were being attacked for their faith and that any fighting that they did, any further terrorist attacks, would be to defend themselves and their way of life. Do you agree with them or do you think that they were missing the point?

The initial fighting was over by early December, when the last city was taken over by the Coalition forces. The Taliban had dispersed into the general population without surrendering. Al-Qaeda was chased into the mountains, and many members were forced to run away from Afghanistan into nearby Pakistan. On December 7, 2004, Hamid Karzai was voted to be the first democratically elected President of Afghanistan, a position which he still holds today. It looked like things were going well.

[34] Quotation source: http://news.bbc.co.uk/

The first democratically elected President of Afghanistan, Hamid Karzai[35]

But then, in 2006, things started to get complicated again. The Taliban began to get back together and started to fight back against the Coalition forces, made up primarily of Afghan, American, and British soldiers. The war became a type of Guerilla warfare where the fighting happened in the streets of the cities and in the distant mountains and caves. The soldiers had to be on the lookout constantly to make sure that no enemies were shooting at them from abandoned buildings and villages. Sometimes, they look for something called a "combat indicator", which were signs that a fight was about to happen. Sometimes that meant groups of people running away from a certain area when they saw Taliban and Coalition soldiers marching towards each other.

Villagers run away from a village full of Taliban soldiers, a sign that there is about to be fighting[36]

[35] Image source: http://www.switchedreality.com/
[36] Image source: http://www.youtube.com/

The troops have learned to be prepared for sneak attacks and have helped to train the local Afghan military and police to take over in fighting against the Taliban. Even so, it is not a rare thing to hear in the news about Americans dying in Afghanistan due to car bombs Taliban attacks, or helicopter accidents. It is still a dangerous place to be.

Chapter 4: What Was It Like to Be a Kid During the War in Afghanistan?

Can you imagine what it would have been like to be a kid living in Afghanistan during all of these events? First off, you would have been genuinely worried about your family when the Taliban was in charge. Do you remember some of the bad things that they did to other people when they were the bosses?

One of the worst things was the way that women were treated. Young girls didn't always get to go to school, and grown women couldn't leave the house unless they were accompanied by a man. Also, many of the women had to thoroughly cover themselves, and if they showed their faces in public they were punished by being beaten with a stick.

The Taliban had a specific way on understanding the Islamic religion, and as President Bush said, if you disobeyed the rules that they made you might get killed. Would you have liked to have lived in a government like that? Of course not! No one wants to have their freedom of choice taken away!

But the problems didn't end when the United States and Coalition forces moved in. Instead of living under an oppressive government, kids now had to see what it was like to live in a war zone. They had to worry about bullets coming through the walls and bombing being dropped on nearby buildings. They had to see people from faraway lands marching down their streets and sometimes they had to run away from their houses and villages with nothing but the clothes in their backs. During the War in Afghanistan, millions of people left the country because it was just plain too dangerous to live there.

Two Afghan children flee their village from the Taliban fighters that took it over[37]

What would you have thought about the War in Afghanistan if you were a kid living there? Well, you might be like Osama Bin Laden who thought that the Americans and others were attacking your religion, or you might be like many other Afghan people who were happy to have someone from the outside come in and make their country more stable and to help it take steps to have a better government.

---

[37] Image source: http://www.youtube.com/

Chapter 5: How Did the War in Afghanistan End?

In this section, we can't actually talk about how the War in Afghanistan ended, because the fighting is still going on. However, we can talk about how the fighting has changed and how it is coming to an end/ We can also talk about what plans the Coalition and Afghan governments have in order to bring an end to foreign action in the area.

Although Presidents Bush and Obama have thought that it was necessary to send in more troops at different times throughout the war, in recent months there has been talk about "troop withdrawal". The Presidents of the United States and Afghanistan, along with the Prime Minister of Great Britain, have the final goal of making sure that Afghanistan is a strong and independent nation that won't fall under the control of extremists like the Taliban ever again.

In order to make that happen, the Coalition forces decided to give the new Afghan government control of the country piece by piece. Starting in the spring of 2013, control over all prisons and prisoners was to be given over to the Afghan people. By the end of 2014, the handover will be complete and all Coalition troops (who have been under the control of NATO since 2003) will be able to go home, their mission accomplished.

In the meantime, President Karzai has tried to make contact with Taliban leaders living in Pakistan and other areas to try and make peace with them, but his efforts haven't been successful. But the lower amount of fighting and improved laws have helped millions of Afghan people living in other countries to come home and start to repair the economy and other parts of the country.

The Afghan people are learning how to work together to make their country better, and knowing that, by 2014, there will be no more NATO troops, they are taking steps to be prepared to keep fighting against the Taliban and other people who want to make the country a worse place. In fact, there are now female soldiers working side by side with male soldiers, and they are helping to find and identify Taliban fighters hiding in houses and neighborhoods. Their work makes the cities in Afghanistan safer for everyone involved.

Individual villages are getting together small groups of soldiers who are ready to fight the Taliban if they should ever come back. One man, named Safer Mohammad, spoke about trying to stop some members of the Taliban from taking away his son. He told the story of how it happened:

> "Four men pushed me to the ground and started beating me. At this moment my other son came out of the house and started firing at them. We had an old rifle from the time of the jihad and we managed to chase off eight Taliban with it…They demanded food, money and accommodation, and they brought nothing good for the residents. Now these have made up their minds: they will ~~not shelter them again~~ or even allow them in the area."[38]

[38] Quotation source: http://www.afghanistan-today.org/

Safer Mohammed and his family fought back against the Taliban[39]

The Taliban and even Al-Qaeda no longer have a strong influence over the people of Afghanistan, and although they may try to do bad things to their enemies, they are constantly being chased down by the good guys and are having a hard time carrying out their plans. As the story of Safer Mohammed shows, the Afghan people are not willing to be bossed around by bad leaders anymore.

The War in Afghanistan is almost over, and it looks like it has been successful.

---

[39] Image source: http://www.afghanistan-today.org/

Chapter 6: What Happened After the War in Afghanistan?

Although there is still some fighting going on, things truly have changed since the Taliban was in charge and the U.S.-led Coalition invaded Afghanistan in 2001. While not everything is perfect, some important steps have been taken towards important goals. Like what?

The first has to do with the improved conditions of several groups within the country. Before, women were mistreated, but now they have much more freedom than before. As we saw, some of them have even started to fight alongside male Afghans to protect their country from the Taliban! Also, many young girls now have the opportunity to go to school. Before the 2001 invasion, only 50,000 girls in the *whole* country were going to school, but today there are almost three million girls going to school! Isn't that great!

Also, although the economy is not as great as it could be, there aren't people starving in the streets like before. Due to a combination of charity and hard work from the Afghan people themselves, the country is starting to take care of the needs of its entire people.

Afghanistan is recovering from all the damage after years of war[40]

Of course, that's not to say that everything has been super smooth and problem free. In February of 2012, some U.S. soldiers on a military base in Afghanistan accidentally burnt some copies of the Islamic holy book, called the Quran. They thought that they were burning terrorist literature with secret messages on it, but by the time they realized their mistake it was too late. The burning of the holy book by people of a different faith was too much for some Afghan people and in protests outside the base thousands of angry men shouted and told the Americans to go home. Even though it didn't lead to anything major, it showed how quickly a misunderstanding can affect thousands of people.

As the War in Afghanistan winds down, some in the United States and other places have started to wonder if it was the right thing to do in the first place. Some feel that the United States rushed into the war because it was angry about the attacks of 9/11 and that the war itself was actually illegal. Is that the case?

Most of the people who criticize the War in Afghanistan say that President Bush and the other Coalition countries never had the legal authority to attack another nation. Why not? Well, all of the countries (including Afghanistan) are part of the United Nations and have agreed to live by its laws. Among them is Article 51 of the U.N. Charter, which says:

> "Nothing in the present Charter shall impair the inherent right of individual or collective self-defence if an armed attack occurs against a Member of the United Nations, until the Security Council has taken measures necessary to maintain international peace and security. Measures taken by Members in the exercise of this right of self-defence shall be immediately reported to the Security Council and shall not in any way affect the authority and responsibility of the Security Council under the present Charter to take at any time such action as it deems necessary in order to maintain or restore international peace and security."[41]

In other words, even though a country is part of the United Nations, they can always defend themselves if attacked by someone else. The Coalition forces, in particular the United States, felt that they were allowed to fight against Afghanistan because Afghanistan was helping Al-Qaeda, the ones who had attacked American on 9/11. However, other people still think that because it wasn't the *government* of Afghanistan that ordered the attacks then the war was illegal and should never have happened.

Although it is too late to change anything or to undo all of the damage done by the war; what do you think? Was it right of the U.S. to invade Afghanistan to stop the Taliban and Al-Qaeda or should they have found a different way to solve the problem?

---

[41] Quotation source: http://www.un.org/

Conclusion

The War in Afghanistan was a important time in the history of everyone involved. Thousands of people died, entire governments were replaced, and justice was served on some men who had done some bad things. Did you learn something new from this manual? Let's review some of the most important points.

The first section told us more about what led up to the fighting. We looked a little at the history of Afghanistan to find out how such bad guys like the Taliban could ever become the ruling party in the country. Do you remember how when the Taliban first arrived it looked like they were going to help the people? How disappointed many Afghans must have felt when they realized that the Taliban were just going to hurt them and take advantage of them like so many others had before.

Then, in the next section, we saw why the war itself actually happened. Although things had been bad in Afghanistan for a while, why did the United Nations decide to get involved in 2001? The answer had a lot to do with the terrorist attack of September 11, 2001, and with a lot of strong emotions. After the World Trade Center and other targets were attacked, the American people wanted to bring to justice anyone who had been involved in the planning of the attacks. Once they found out that Al-Qaeda was the group that had organized everything, they were determined to make sure that the members of Al-Qaeda paid for their crimes.

Even though Al-Qaeda was being protected by another country (Afghanistan) President Bush made it clear that anyone who helped the bad guys was like a bad guy himself. So because the Taliban helped Al-Qaeda and protected them from punishment, the Coalition felt that the Taliban had to go too.

Then, we saw some of the interesting details of how the war was fought. The beginning was pretty standard, but the final part has been difficult and the NATO (North Atlantic Treaty Organization) troops are still having a tough time doing their job and keeping the region stable and safe. They have to fight small groups of soldiers who hide in the mountains and in villages, and the fighting never seems to stop. Along with the bravery of the NATO troops, we also saw how many Afghan men and women have been affected by the war and how they have helped to fight against the bad guys.

The section after that showed us what it would be like to be a kid living in Afghanistan during the war. Daily life was changed in many ways from before the war; sometimes in a good way and sometimes in a bad way. Little boys and girls get to go to school now, but some of them are still scared that they wil be hurt in the fighting and some of them are still quite poor.

Then, the next section talked about how the war started to wind down what the plans are for keeping the peace after the NATO troops leave in 2014. The final section talked about what major changes Afghanistan has seen since it started. It was nice to see how the Afghan people are taking seriously their new job of keeping the peace in their country and how even women are joining in the fighting.
We also saw in this section that some people think that the war was and still is illegal and that no one should have fought it. What do you think: are they, right?

The War in Afghanistan was fought in a faraway country, but it was meant to protect people living in the United States. Do you feel safer knowing that the members of Al-Qaeda aren't as strong as they were before and that it is harder for them to organize and carry out their terrorist attacks? The United States has not had a major terrorist attack on its soil since 2001, and there is no doubt that at least part of the credit goes to the brave men and women who have fought and who keep fighting in Afghanistan.

The future looks bright for Afghanistan as its people are learning to be a part of the international community and to stand up for what is right, even if it isn't always easy. The war that began in 2001 helped them to take their first steps away from a being a dangerous country and towards being one that provides a safe and healthy environment for its entire people.

The Iraq War
A History Just for Kids

Troops in Iraq get ready to fight[42]

---

[42] Image source: http://www.guardian.co.uk/politics/2009/feb/25/cabinet-minutes-iraq-war

Introduction

Freddy Watkins was a private in the United States Marine Corps. Born and raised in Indiana, U.S.A., he knew since he was a kid that he wanted to be a soldier when he grew up. When he played war with his friends, it wasn't a game for him; it was training. All during high school he tried to exercise and eat well so that he could qualify for basic training with the Marines. And the day after graduation, when he turned 18, he went with his parents to the local recruiting center and signed up to join the Marine Corps.

Basic training had been tough, but he had passed, along with most of his team. Shortly after graduation, he and his unit were assigned to Kuwait. No one knew exactly why they were there, but everyone knew that something important was going to happen soon. Troops from around the country were being sent to Kuwait and massed together on the border with Iraq. After the terrorist attacks of September 11th, lots of guys like him had joined the ranks of the military to hunt down the bad guys and to bring them to justice. Whenever Freddy thought about the twin towers falling, and all of those people who died, his blood boiled and he started to tingle all over. A lot of people got sad when they thought about September 11th; but not Freddy, Freddy just got mad.

In March of this year, Freddy and the rest of his unit were told to move north into Iraq. This was the first time that most of the men had experienced real combat, and it was pretty scary. There were planes flying overhead dropping bombs, tanks in front of them clearing the roads, and large trucks that carried him and his fellow soldiers from one village to the next, arresting enemy fighters and sometimes getting into firefights with them.

Now, here he was in Baghdad. The Iraqi government had been overthrown already, and the mission of Freddy and his men was to maintain the security in Iraq's capital city. He was to patrol the borders of the area known as the "Green Zone" and make sure that no Iraqi rebels attacked the new military and governmental headquarters in the country. Freddy shuttered as he thought about some of the ways that Iraqi rebels fought. Because they had older weapons, less money, and smaller numbers than the Americans and British, they used their imaginations to cause all kinds of problems. Sometimes they had snipers shoot at the American soldiers without any warning, sometimes they attacked at night, and sometimes they put bombs inside of cars and drove them right through the checkpoints around the edge of the Green Zone.

But the weapon that had killed some of Freddy's men was something called an IED, an Improvised Explosive Device. IEDs were kind of like homemade bombs that were hard to see. Sometimes they were buried in the sand and sometimes they were hidden under large pieces of garbage on the side of the road. When the soldiers went out of the Green Zone and into the city, they traveled in long lines of trucks and armored cars called "convoys". Every time that they saw something on the side of the road everyone would hold their breath, wondering if it was a bomb. Sometimes cars pulled up next to them, and the passengers started to shoot large guns, and sometimes they heard gunshots but couldn't see where they were coming from.

The result was that Freddy and his men were nervous all the time. Every Iraqi that they saw might be an enemy, every pile of garbage might be a bomb, and every *pop* might be the bullet that kills them. Freddy couldn't sleep at night; he had so many nightmares. He felt like he couldn't trust anyone who wasn't an American, not even the Iraqis that were on his side. He had heard that some soldiers were going home because of the stress and that a few had even committed suicide, and Freddy wondered where he would be in six more months. His unit wasn't scheduled to go home until then.

Together with a group of three soldiers, Freddy held his gun and squinted against the sun. Iraq was under control of the Americans, but it sure didn't feel like the fighting was going to stop anytime soon. That meant that Freddy had a job to do. It wasn't easy, and it might not be popular, but it was his job. Taking a deep breath Freddy gave the order to move out, and he and his men walked along the Green Zone border to keep the people inside safe.

The Iraq War was different from other wars before it. For most of the war, there were no clear battle lines, no clear military goals, and it wasn't always easy to know who your friends were and who your enemies were. The world community wasn't sure whether or not to support the war, and it seemed like the fighting just never stopped. Some people compared it to the Vietnam War, which was a war famous for its violence and for the lack of communication between the two sides.

In this book, we will be taking a closer look at the Iraq War, which was fought from 2003-2011. Almost 4,500 American soldiers died during the war, and another 33,000 were wounded. Over 110,000 Iraqis, both soldiers and civilians, would eventually die in the fighting also. But do you know what led up to the war? In the next chapter, we will see how the Gulf War, fought in 1991, planted the seeds of the Iraq War. Specifically, the war that Saddam Hussein chose to deal with the international community caused serious problems and made other nations want to invade his country.

Then we will see why the war happened. In his speech just before the Iraq War began, President George W. Bush explained the main reasons for the bombing and invasion of Iraq. We will look at each of the reasons one by one, and you can decide for yourself whether or not you agree with them and whether or not you think it was a good idea to invade Iraq.

Then we will see what happened during the war. We will see that the war was divided up into two phases: the initial combat phase and then the rebuilding phase. The rebuilding phase is what took the longest and was the most difficult. The fighting in Iraq seemed to go on and on, and as American soldiers kept dying in the fighting, people back home in the United States started to think that the war was not such a brilliant idea after all. Several stories that came out in the news made some Americans think that the White House was not truly doing a good job in Iraq at all. Also, we will see that the use of private citizens to rebuild Iraq was unpopular with some Americans and even led to some problems.

Then we will see what it was like to be a kid during the Iraq War. Whether you were a kid living in Iraq during the fighting or were back in the United States learning about it in school, you would have been sure to have had an opinion about all the fighting and violence. Also, people that you knew and loved would have been affected by the war, something decided by people in an office far away.

Then we will learn about how the Iraq War ended. After a long time, the rebuilding phase finally came to a close, and the American troops left Iraq. Were they successful in their mission to leave Iraq a better place than they found it? The following chapter will show us what Iraq is like today and how many people view the 2003 Iraq War.

Your parents probably remember the Iraq War quite well, so why not ask them to talk about as you read through this book. That way, you may be able to learn about what their life was like back then and what they thought about the war. Are you ready to learn more? Great! Let's get started.

Chapter 1: What Led Up To the Iraq War?

Most people don't like war; war is expensive, a lot of people get hurt and die, and long friendships with other countries can get ruined practically overnight. Most nations try to use what's called *diplomacy* to avoid fighting. They have ambassadors to represent their leaders, they have representatives go the organizations like the United Nations, where nations can talk out their problems, and they have secret communications to solve small issues before they get bigger. There are also other methods of keeping bad countries from becoming worse: for example, economic sanctions (punishments) make sure that bad countries can't do business with anyone, and so they lose lots of money. Most countries, when they have to experience economic sanctions, decide to stop doing the bad things that made everyone so angry. But sometimes, diplomacy, meetings in the United Nations, economic sanctions, and even secret communications can't stop some bad leader from doing bad things. In those rare situations, sometimes a war has to happen.

For United States President George W. Bush and British Prime Minister Tony Blair, the 2003 Iraq War was just such a situation. But what kinds of things had happened that made them feel that way? Let's find out.

In 1980, Iraq invaded the neighboring nation of Iran and, for eight years, fought a long and bloody war. During that war, the Iraqi president, Saddam Hussein, used awful chemical weapons against the Iranian people, killing many thousands of them. The war ended in 1988, but two years later President Saddam Hussein invaded another neighboring nation, called Kuwait, and took it over. The Kuwaiti people were treated badly by the Iraqi military, and it looked like President Hussein might keep attacking other nations, including Saudi Arabia, who provided oil for much of the world. In the United Nations, it was decided to go to war against Iraq and a large group of countries (called "The Coalition") got together to fight the war. In less than two months, the Coalition had won. Saddam Hussein removed his troops from Kuwait and promised to allow United Nations weapons inspectors into his country to make sure that there were no dangerous chemical, nuclear, or biological weapons. Because they could hurt so many people, both soldiers and innocent civilians, their weapons were called Weapons of Mass Destruction.

After the 1980 war with Iran and the 1991 war against the Coalition (called the Gulf War) many of the people of Iraq thought that it was time to have a new leader in their country. In the North and in the South, groups of Iraqi people tried to rise up against Saddam Hussein and to force him to stop being president. However, instead of listening to what the people of his country wanted, President Hussein killed anyone who tried to stop him. Tens of thousands of people, mostly innocent civilians, were killed by their own president as they expressed their views. The world was shocked to see how Saddam Hussein treated his own people, people of his own country.

Saddam Hussein was a strict leader and didn't allow any rebellion[43]

In the meantime, the United Nations inspectors weren't having an easy time doing their job in Iraq. As we saw earlier, part of the condition of ending the Gulf War was that Saddam would allow U.N. inspectors into his country to make sure that he wasn't making or using any Weapons of Mass Destruction and that any older weapons that he had were being destroyed. But the inspectors didn't always feel welcome in Iraq, weren't always allowed to go anywhere they wanted, and sometimes they weren't even allowed across the border.

The world saw what was happening in Iraq, and because the Iraqi government (led by Saddam Hussein) wasn't keeping up their end of the bargain they agreed to during the Gulf War and they weren't cooperating fully with the United Nations, the United Stated (under President Bill Clinton) and Great Britain (under Prime Minister Tony Blair) decided to start a four day bombing campaign of key targets in Iraq. Called "Operation Desert Fox", the attacks took place from December 16-19, 1998. Over 600 Iraqi people died in the bombings and Iraq realized how serious the situation was. But, despite the threats and the bombings, Saddam Hussein was not willing to cooperate with the rest of the world and became more angry and stubborn. News reports made it clear that Iraq would no longer allow any United Nations inspectors inside its borders ever again.

Around this time, the Unites States started to receive some pretty worrying reports from their spies. Called "intelligence", these reports made it look like Iraq was still producing Weapons of Mass Destruction and that some of them might even be nuclear. In the news and in front of different governmental meetings, the American people heard about all of the damage that these weapons could do, how many Americans could die, and how dangerous Iraq, and in particular Saddam Hussein, still

[43] Image source: http://www.biography.com/people/saddam-hussein-9347918

Secretary of State Colin Powell went before the United Nations to explain how serious the Weapons of Mass Destruction in Iraq truly were[44]

Some of the reports made it seem like bombs and explosions, and American deaths seemed a long ways off. Problems in the Middle East were so far away that it seemed almost like watching a movie and not real life. A lot of Americans heard the scary reports but didn't actually take them very seriously; that is, they didn't until September 11, 2001.

Do you remember the terrorist attacks of September 11, 2001? Do you remember where you were and what you were doing? If you were too little, why not ask your parents of other adults that you may know what they remember from that day? On September 11, four planes were stolen from airports on the East Coast and were used like giant missiles to attack the World Trade Center building, the Pentagon, and a target in Washington D.C. The plane headed towards Washington D.C. never made it because some brave passengers fought against the terrorists, and the plane crash landed in a rural area of Pennsylvania.

The American people, and truly the whole world, were shocked at what happened on September the 11th. Just 19 men, smaller than any army in any country, were able to cause so much damage and pain to so many people. Americans and the White House began to think about terrorism more seriously and to realize that terrorists had to be stopped before they made it to the United States.

[44] Image source: http://news.xin.msn.com/en/silverlight-gallery.aspx?cp-documentid=5225258&page=15

The Twin Towers were destroyed on September 11, and thousands of innocent people died[45]

As it tends to happen after a lot of tragedies, there was a lot of confusion and misunderstandings flying around after the attacks of September 11th. One of the news reports that was repeated man times was that Iraq had supported the terrorist group (Al-Qaeda) that had carried out the attack on 9/11. For the White House, hearing that Iraq, whom they already suspected of making and storing Weapons of Mass Destruction, had been somehow connected to the attacks of September 11th was too much. They thought that Iraq had to be stopped and that it was causing too much trouble to too many people.

The United Nations agreed that something had to be done and that the economic sanctions that they had been using didn't seem to be working. So, the U.N. Security Council sent out Resolution 1441 on November 8, 2002. The resolution gave Iraq one more chance to live up to the terms of its surrender from 1991, to stop buying and making dangerous weapons, and to pay to Kuwait the money they owed them from the Gulf War attacks. The representatives who wrote the resolution were careful not to make it look like war would automatically follow if Saddam didn't obey. In fact, Saddam did agree to let the U.N. inspectors back in after the resolution was passed. However, the United States didn't think that he was serious but that he was playing political games to buy a little bit of time.

By early 2003, the United States was getting impatient. Even though some people thought that Iraq was doing more to cooperate with the United Nations orders, others didn't think that they were doing enough and that they were hiding something. President Bush insisted that Iraq was still violating the terms of the Resolution and that the Security Council should meet together again to decide what to do. France promised not to support any action leading to war, and the United States and the United Kingdom insisted that war was the only way to stop Saddam Hussein and his dangerous government. A deadline was set by the U.S. and the U.K. on March 17, 2003, to cooperate 100% with the U.N. standards. They gave Iraq just 48 hours to act.

[45] Image source: http://e29backroad.blogspot.com/2012/11/911-first-person-account_16.html

The United Nations wanted to give Iraq more time, but the U.S. and U.K. didn't want to wait. Without the permission of their fellow leaders, these two nations started to build up large numbers of troops in Kuwait to prepare for bombing and an invasion of Iraq. On March 20, 2003, after the 48 hour deadline had come and gone, a massive bombing campaign, called a "Shock and Awe" campaign, was launched in order to weaken main Iraqi targets. At the same time, the soldiers in Kuwait invaded from the south and Iraqis trained by the CIA in the North began to move towards the capital city of Baghdad. The fighting started quickly at about 5:30 in the morning and got serious quickly.

The Iraq War had officially begun.

Chapter 2: Why Did the Iraq War Happen?

As we saw earlier, no one actually ever wants a war. But sometimes, when all the other options have been tried, a war can't be avoided. For U.S. President Bush and U.K. Prime Minister Blair, they had tried all of the peaceful solutions but Iraq was still too dangerous to be left alone. On March 20, 2003, these two men started the Iraq War. But what were their main reasons for doing so? Although they were many reasons given to the American public and given to the world community, a speech that President Bush gave on March 19, 2003 lays out his reasons for thinking that the Iraq War was needed.

President Bush talked about the invasion of Iraq on March 19, 2003[46]

Let's see what President Bush said in that important speech.

> "My fellow citizens, at this hour, American and coalition forces are in the early stages of military operations to disarm Iraq, to free its people and to defend the world from grave danger...To all the men and women of the United States Armed Forces now in the Middle East, the peace of a troubled world and the hopes of an oppressed people now depend on you...I want Americans and all the world to know that coalition forces will make every effort to spare innocent civilians from harm. A campaign on the harsh terrain of a nation as large as California could be longer and more difficult than some predict. And helping Iraqis achieve a united, stable and free country will require our sustained commitment.
>
> We come to Iraq with respect for its citizens, for their illustrious civilization and for the religious faiths they practice. We have no ambition in Iraq, except to remove a threat and restore control of that country to its own people...Our nation enters this conflict reluctantly -- yet, our purpose is sure. The people of the United States and our friends and allies will not live at the mercy of an outlaw regime that threatens the peace with weapons of mass murder. We will meet that threat now, with our Army, Air Force, Navy, Coast Guard and Marines, so that we do not have to meet it later with armies of fire fighters and police and doctors on the streets of our cities...My fellow citizens, the dangers to our country and the world will be overcome. We will pass through this

time of peril and carry on the work of peace. We will defend our freedom. We will bring freedom to others and we will prevail."[47]

This speech was important because it was the first that many Americans had heard about the invasion of Iraq. President Bush wanted everyone to understand why the government had decided to send troops to fight in Iraq and why they should support the war effort. Did you see the reasons that were given to the American public? Do you see the clear connection with the terrorist attacks of September 11th? Let's highlight a few of the most important sentences.

- **"American and coalition forces are in the early stages of military operations to disarm Iraq, to free its people and to defend the world from grave danger."** This sentence clearly explains what the United States and United Kingdom wanted to achieve by invading Iraq. They wanted to take care of the whole Weapons of Mass Destruction (WMD) problem. They wanted the replace Saddam Hussein as president, because he was such a cruel person. And they wanted to stop Iraq from supporting terrorist groups like Al-Qaeda.

Those three goals were the whole reason that the Iraq War was fought. Do they sound like good reasons to you? They sounded pretty good to most Americans back in 2003. But does it surprise you that France and many other nations did not support the Iraq War? If there were such solid reasons to invade Iraq, why didn't everyone get involved, like they had in previous wars? We will learn later that of the three reasons used to invade Iraq, two of them weren't actually true at all! Some nations were worried that might be the case and wanted to investigate more, but the United States and Great Britain were worried that waiting longer might mean more deaths and so were eager to get Saddam Hussein and his government out of power.

However, did you note another fascinating quote from the speech? Check it out below:

- **"The people of the United States and our friends and allies will not live at the mercy of an outlaw regime that threatens the peace with weapons of mass murder. We will meet that threat now, with our Army, Air Force, Navy, Coast Guard and Marines, so that we do not have to meet it later with armies of fire fighters and police and doctors on the streets of our cities."** What do you think President Bush was talking about when he mentioned fire fighters, police, and doctors fighting a war on the streets of our cities? There can be no doubt: President Bush was talking about the attacks of September 11th. Right or wrong, he felt that invading Iraq would stop future terrorist attacks in the Unites States.

Some people accused President Bush of using peoples' emotions and fear to gain support for the war, and maybe they are right. Either way, many Americans thought, and continue to think, that the invasion of Iraq was directly related to the attacks of 9/11. Do you agree with them? Do you think it was right to connect the two events?

In other speeches and conferences, President Bush also made it clear that he wanted to invade Iraq because of its human rights violations. Do you know what human rights are? The phrase "human rights" refers to the things that anybody should be allowed to do, like have a job, live peacefully, and not be afraid of the government. In Iraq, anyone who disagreed with the government quickly found themselves in a lot of trouble so it could be said that Saddam was violating the human rights of his citizens. Like we saw in the above quotation, President Bush wanted to free the people of Iraq and give them back their country. Instead of living under a tyrant (a bad leader) he wanted to let them be a government like the United States, where people can choose their own presidents and make their own laws.

As you can see, the Iraq War happened to protect both the Iraqi people from a dangerous leader and Americans from his weapons and from any future terrorist attacks. While some of the reasons ended up being wrong, at the time the war was supported by a large group of Americans and British citizens, although other countries thought that it was a bad idea.

Chapter 3: What Happened During the Iraq War?

The Iraq War received a special mission name: Operation Iraqi Freedom. The name of the mission was to remind everyone what the American and British militaries were fighting for. They were fighting together with the Iraqi people to get rid of a tyrannical leader and a bad government. That was the idea.

Operation Iraqi Freedom started with smart bombs being launched against important building in the capital city of Baghdad. Most people who were watching the war from far away thought that the war would be similar to the 1991 Gulf War, where a long period of bombing was followed by a short invasion. Imagine their surprise when they learned that American and British soldiers invaded Iraq right after the bombing started. The huge number of bombs falling from the sky and the large amount of soldiers (over 200,000 troops) invading from the south were meant to scare the Iraqis into not fighting. And it seems like the tactic worked.

The Iraqi military surprised the Coalition troops by not using a "scorched earth" policy. Have you ever heard of a scorched earth policy before? It is where one army destroys everything as they run away so that the other side cannot use it to get stronger. Sometimes, this means destroying bridges, roads, houses, crops, and even killing animals so that they can't be eaten. During the 1991 Gulf War, the Iraqi troops set fire to more than 600 oil wells as they left Kuwait and caused a lot of problems for the other side. Everyone thought that the Iraqi would do the same thing in 2003, but most of them just surrendered, and the Coalition troops were able to move forward quickly. By March 25, they were only 60 miles outside of Baghdad.

An enormous dust storm made everyone slow down a little bit and so there was a bit of a pause in the fighting.

A soldier took a picture of a 2003 dust storm in Iraq. Can you see why everyone had to stop fighting?

But the pause didn't last too long. Within a short time, the guns were making noise again and the Coalition troops kept pushing forward towards the capital city. On April 4, the Baghdad airport was captured, and on April 9 the entire city was under American control. That same day, a major city named Basra in the south of the country was captured by British forces. The government and leaders of Iraq had since run away, and no one knew where they were.

On April 13, 2003, there was a real victory when Saddam Hussein's hometown of Tikrit was captured by American forces. Although several smaller areas had to be brought under control and borders had to be set up and protected, it looked like Operation Iraqi Freedom was going to be a success. In fact, on May 1, President Bush visited the *USS Abraham Lincoln*, an aircraft carrier that had just returned from battle in the Persian Gulf area. After making an impressive landing aboard an airplane, he gave an exciting speech with a large banner behind him that said "Mission Accomplished".

President Bush during his "Mission Accomplished" speech[49]

Why did the banner say "Mission Accomplished" if there was still fighting going on? The speech given by President Bush was meant to show that Iraq was now under control of the Coalition but that there was still some rebuilding work to do and that Saddam Hussein still had to be found. However, many people were upset when they saw the banner. Have a look at a few excerpts from the speech to see if you can find out why:

> "My fellow Americans, major combat operations in Iraq have ended. In the battle of Iraq, the United States and our allies have prevailed. And now our coalition is engaged in securing and reconstructing that country…We have difficult work to do in Iraq. We're bringing order to parts of that country that remain dangerous. We're pursuing and finding leaders of the old regime who will be held to account for their crimes. We've begun the search for hidden chemical and biological weapons, and already know of hundreds of sites that will be investigated. We are helping to rebuild Iraq where the dictator built palaces for himself instead of hospitals and schools…The transition from dictatorship to democracy will take time, but it is worth every effort. Our coalition will stay until our work is done and then we will leave and we will leave behind a free Iraq."[50]

Can you understand why some people got upset when they saw the banner and heard the speech? Some people thought that President Bush was saying that the dangerous part of the war was over and that everyone should celebrate. Of course, in his speech the President made it clear that there would still be work to do, but it seems like no one knew just how dangerous Iraq actually was. At the time the speech was given, 141 Americans had been killed in the fighting. But before the war would finally end in 2011 (eight years later) 4,347 more would be killed. In other words, almost 97% of the soldiers killed in Iraq would die after the President had said "Mission Accomplished".

The challenge after taking over the city, as the President had said, would be to rebuild Iraq. Schools, hospitals, and governmental offices had to be built, and local Iraqis had to be trained as politicians, policemen, and as soldiers. The idea was to teach the Iraqis how to take care of their own country, without Saddam Hussein bossing them around. But after the bad leaders and the bad governments disappeared, something unexpected happened: the Iraqi people couldn't decide who they wanted to be their leader and they started a civil war. One side wanted the Americans to help, and the other side wanted the Americans to leave Iraq right away. The ones who wanted the Americans to leave and who were unhappy with the new Iraqi government being put together were called "insurgents", or rebels.

The insurgents were fewer in number and didn't have the same weapons or money to fight as the Coalition troops did. So instead of fighting a traditional war, the insurgents would use car bombs, traps, and snipers to attack American and British troops before running away. Some insurgents would even hide bombs under their clothing, walk to a crowded marketplace or military checkpoint, and then detonate the bomb to kill themselves and everyone around them. Lots of soldiers were wounded and killed this way. Those who survived often went home missing and arm or a leg. The fighting was dangerous and scary.

There was a bright spot during all of the tense fighting when Saddam Hussein was discovered hiding in a small hole on December 13, 2003. The hole was dug on a farmhouse hear his hometown of Tikrit. Saddam had some money with him, but it was clear that he had been hiding for a long time. He looked different than he had when he was in power.

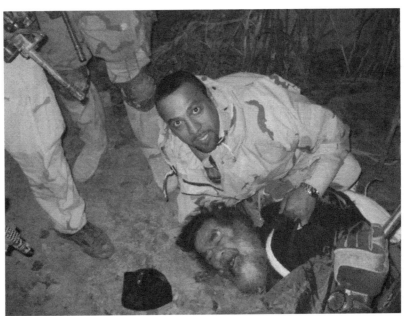

This picture of Saddam Hussein was taken moments after he was pulled out of his hiding place[51]

There was a trial in an Iraqi court, and on December 30, 2006, he was executed by his own people for all the bad things he had done and crimes he had committed during his time as president. But although Saddam had been executed, the fighting went on in Iraq.

Because things didn't look like they were getting any better, during January and February of 2007, President Bush decided to send 20,000 more troops to Iraq, mainly to the city of Baghdad, to get the situation under control. After surviving many more attacks by insurgents, which seemed to kill Americans almost every day, new U.S. President Barack Obama announced a "drawdown" of troops in Iraq that would begin in 2010. By August, all but 50,000 troops had left, and the mission was no longer about fighting, but providing stability to the country. The Coalition wanted to Iraqis to fight their own civil war and to solve their own problems, and the Americans would only be there to help a little while longer before leaving.

The Iraq War lasted over eight years from start to finish. At first, many Americans agreed that U.S. soldiers should go and fight in that war. However, as time went by, their opinions started to change. What kind of things influenced their opinions?

One key factor was the news. News reports of the terrible fighting and slow progress made some people think that all of those American soldiers were dying for nothing. Other news reports talked about how Americans were mistreating Iraqi prisoners, and it made the situation look like it was getting out of control. Also, some 100,000 "Private Military Contractors" were hired by the United States to go to Iraq and work in different areas. Some worked in construction, some worked in security, and some actually participated in the fighting. But as reports surfaced of these contractors becoming violent with Iraqi citizens, more and more Americans decided that they thought that the Iraq War had been a lousy idea, or at the very best that it had not been handled well by the White House.

The Iraq War was becoming unpopular with everyone involved, even the politicians and the soldiers.

Chapter 4: What Was It Like To Be a Kid During the Iraq War?

A child sits on tops of a ruined building in Iraq[52]

Have you ever heard the sound of a gunshot or seen fireworks light up the sky? Depending on the circumstances, those things can be cool and exciting. But imagine those same types of explosions in your neighborhood, destroying houses and killing people you know and love. Seems a lot scarier, right?

In Iraq, kids saw the world around them crumble and fall apart. Their president, their community, their schools, their friends…everything changed almost overnight. It wasn't strange to see dead bodies (both Iraqi and American) in the streets or to have to listen to people crying over family members that had been killed.

As a kid, sometimes war is hard to understand. You wonder why everyone can't just stop fighting and talk about their problems, like you do with your friends at school. You can't understand why anyone would use bombs and guns to get their way. At school, they tell us that fighting is bad, so it's strange to see grown-ups doing what kids aren't allowed to. During the Iraq War, lots of kids had to listen to the bombs and wonder if the next one was going to fall on their house. They were scared to go to the store because of the insurgents and their bombs, so it seemed like there was no safe place to go. Can you imagine being scared all the time? What do you think life will be like for those kids when they grow up?

Even though the war has since ended, you can imagine how some of those kids still have distressing dreams and feel sad about everything that happened.

In the United States kids saw the Iraq War on TV and then later saw the veterans coming home with injuries and sad looks on their faces. Even though they were never worried about dying in a war, do you ~~think that American kids got s~~ad when they thought about it too?

[52] Image source: http://thesituationist.wordpress.com/2007/06/28/our-soldiers-their-children-the-lasting-impact-of-the-war-in-iraq/

American kids could have talked to their parents to try and understand what was happening. They could have asked why the war was happening and what it all meant. Even though their parents might not have all the answers, kids would at least get to think a little about what was happening and why. And when they saw the news reports about how awful things were over there and how many people were dying, you can be sure that some kids got pretty sad.

War is hard on everybody, but kids are the ones who can't really run away or do anything about it. In other words, it's no good to be a kid during a war.

Chapter 5: How Did the Iraq War End?

For years, the fighting had been fierce in Iraq. During regular patrols soldiers would be ambushed by insurgents or would worry about running over a bomb and dying or being captured. Then suddenly, President Obama announced a troop drawdown and by August 2010 there were only 50,000 soldiers left who would work primarily as trainers and peacekeepers. Then, on December 15, 2011, a small ceremony was held in Baghdad and the last fighting soldiers left Iraq (although a few thousand stayed behind on permanent bases).

From such a tremendous start to such a quiet finish, the Iraq War surprised people at every turn. Some people were expecting momentous speeches or fireworks, but it all ended when the U.S. government realized that the civil war in Iraq was not going to be solved with American guns. After having made sure that there were no more Weapons of Mass Destruction in Iraq, that Saddam Hussein was no longer in power, and that the Iraqi people were free to decided how they wanted their country to be run, President Obama decided that the time had come to bring the troops home.

When the soldier left Iraq, they left a country that still had a weak economy, still had some fighting between the religious and political groups, and still had some serious problems.

What happened after the Iraq War?

After the Iraq War ended, the soldiers all went home to the United States and Britain. Some of them began to have serious emotional problems because of all of the stress that they had while in Iraq. Do you remember what it was like day to day in Iraq? The American soldiers never knew when they would be attacked, and sometimes they didn't even know who their friends were and who their enemies were. When they came home, it was hard for some of the soldiers to get used to peacetime. Sometimes they thought that anyone who looked at them strangely was an enemy who wanted to hurt them, and sometimes they even got quite confused and tried to hurt their families.

The situation with the soldiers got them a lot of attention from doctors who found that they were suffering from something called Post Traumatic Stress Disorder (PTSD). With professional help, a lot of the soldiers were able to start to enjoy once more the lives that they had before the war.

In Iraq, the war had stopped but some of the local fighting kept going on. The insurgents still use car bombs to fight and some people are still scared of going to the market or out into the city. Large groups of Iraqi people don't have access to clean water or enough food, so a lot of kids and adults get sick pretty often.

Now, this is a good time to ask yourself a question: are things better or worse for the Iraqi people than they were before? In the past, the Iraqi people suffered from constant war and bad treatment from a mean leader. Since the 2003 Iraq War, have things gotten any better? Well, sadly, not much. The leaders are better in Iraq, but there is still lots of fighting and people still don't have enough food or water.

Worse yet, some of the reasons that were used to start the war turned out to be wrong. Do you remember the three main reasons that President Bush mentioned when he said that the United States was going to war? As we saw earlier, the United States and United Kingdom wanted to:

1. Take care of the whole Weapons of Mass Destruction (WMD) problem.
2. Replace Saddam Hussein as president, because he was such a cruel person.
3. Stop Iraq from supporting terrorist groups like Al-Qaeda.

Well, two of those reasons (the first one and the last one) ended up being wrong. There were no new WMDs ever found in Iraq, and there was no proof that Iraq was making any new ones or that they even had plans to do so. Also, there was never any connection found between the government of Iraq and Al-Qaeda, the group that destroyed the Twin Towers on 9/11.

Looking back, some people feel that the Iraq War was a mistake. They feel that thousands of Americans, Britons, Iraqis, and others died for no reason. They feel that the people of the world were lied to in order to get them to support the war, and that the war itself was not handled well.

Why it is impossible for anyone to know everything at the beginning of a war, do you think that President Bush and Prime Minister Blair should have waited more time before invading Iraq or do you think that they made the right decision with the information that they had? Why not ask some adults that you know what they think about the war and why they have that opinion?

Conclusion

We have learned a lot about the Iraq War in this book. We saw how it began, what happened during it, and how it ended. Do you think that you could share with someone else all that you learned about the war? Let's review some of the most important points together.

In the first chapter, we saw how the Gulf War, fought in 1991, planted the seeds of the Iraq War. Specifically, the war that Saddam Hussein chose to deal with the international community caused serious problems and made other nations want to invade his country. Remember, Saddam Hussein had promised to let international inspectors into his country to look for Weapons of mass Destruction. But when he began to stop letting them in and to make it more difficult for them to do their jobs, the United Nations sent Resolution 1441 to try to force him. When things still moved slowly, the U.S. and U.K. didn't want to wait any longer and invaded Iraq on March 20, 2003.

Then we saw why the war happened. In his speech just before the Iraq War began, President George W. Bush explained the three main reasons for the bombing and invasion of Iraq. We looked at each of the reasons one by one, and you were able to decide for yourself whether or not you agreed with them and whether or not you thought it was a good idea to invade Iraq. Do you remember the three reasons? The Coalition wanted to remove Saddam Hussein from power, wanted to get rid of the WMDs, and wanted to make sure that Iraq stopped supporting terrorist groups like Al-Qaeda. Those were the main reasons for the 2003 Iraq War.

Then we saw what happened during the war. We saw that the war was divided up into two phases: the initial combat phase (which only lasted from March 20 to May 1, 2003) and then the much longer rebuilding phase. The rebuilding phase is what was the most difficult. The fighting in Iraq seemed to go on and on, and as American soldiers kept dying in the fighting, people back home in the United States started to think that the war was not such a brilliant idea after all. They saw that the Iraq invasion had turned into a civil war, and that maybe America shouldn't be involved anymore. Also, we saw the power of the news media. We saw how several stories that came out in the news made some Americans think that the White House was not truly doing a good job in Iraq at all. We also saw that the use of private citizens to rebuild Iraq was unpopular with some Americans and even led to some problems in Iraq.

Then we saw what it was like to be a kid during the Iraq War. Whether you were a kid living in Iraq during the fighting or were back in the United States learning about it in school, you would have been sure to have had an opinion about all the fighting and violence. Also, people that you knew and loved would have been affected by the war, something decided by people in an office far away. Kids often have a hard time understanding wars, and the Iraq War was a confusing time for lots of people- adults included.

Then we learned about how the Iraq War ended. After a long time, the rebuilding phase finally came to a close, and the American troops left Iraq in December 0f 2011. Were they successful in their mission to leave Iraq a better place than they found it? What do you think? We were able to compare Iraq before and after the 2003 invasion, and to be honest, Iraq is still a pretty rough place to live in. The following chapter showed us what Iraq is like today and how most of the people view the 2003 Iraq War. Do you remember what many people think about the war? Many people, both American and Iraqi, think that the war was a lousy idea.

The Iraq War was a time when the United States continued its close relationship with Great Britain and chose to ignore what many other countries were saying. Instead of waiting for the United Nations to give them permission to act (like what had happened in 1991 before the Gulf War) the U.S. and the U.K. decided for themselves what the best course of action was and went ahead with it.

The international community wasn't happy with any part of the Iraq War. While some nations helped out in different ways, others decided not to be such close friends with the United States. In fact, for many people living around the world, the United States became less like a helpful friend and more like a big bully. To this day American politicians still talk about and argue about the Iraq War, and they can't agree on whether or not it was a good idea.

What about you? Well, while you may not be the President of the United States (yet!), do you think that there are any lessons for you to learn after reading this book? Of course there are. One of them has to do with getting all of the information before getting into a fight. Sometime you might hear a rumor and it may not be true at all. Before you get too angry, you should always make sure of the facts. President Bush and Primer Minister Blair didn't have all the facts when they invaded Iraq. If they had known what we know now, maybe things would have been different. So whenever someone tells you something that makes you angry, be sure to make sure that what they said was true.

Also, it is a good idea to learn something from President Obama. When he became president in 2009, the Iraq War had been going on for a long time. However, he knew when it was time to walk away from the fight. He knew that no matter how many more soldiers he sent to Iraq that things weren't going to change that way. You can learn the same lesson: learn when it is time to just walk away from something. Whether you are arguing, fighting, or being bullied, sometimes you know that nothing good will happen if you stick around. So be like President Obama and be smart enough to leave when it is time.

The 2003 Iraq War was a time when the news helped people to see what was happening on the other side of the world almost instantly. There were lots of opinions, and lots of people died- including President Saddam Hussein. What do you think: if you had been old enough, would you have fought in the Iraq War or would you have protested against it? Would you have tried to help the Iraqi people one way or another?

Iraqi boys flash peace signs[53]

---

[53] Image source: http://www.boman12.org/issues-peace.htm